Guarded by a few G.I.s, Germans march into captivity past an American mobile antiaircraft unit near Limburg, 20 miles east of the Rhine in central Germany. These prisoners, who were among the 800 taken by the U.S. First Army in March 1945, joined the 500,000 who had already surrendered to Americans that year.

This volume is one of a series that chronicles
in full the events of the Second World War.

WORLD WAR II · TIME-LIFE BOOKS · ALEXANDRIA, VIRGINIA

BY RONALD H. BAILEY
AND THE EDITORS OF TIME-LIFE BOOKS

PRISONERS OF WAR

Time-Life Books Inc.
is a wholly owned subsidiary of
TIME INCORPORATED

Founder: Henry R. Luce 1898-1967

Editor-in-Chief: Henry Anatole Grunwald
President: J. Richard Munro
Chairman of the Board: Ralph P. Davidson
Executive Vice President: Clifford J. Grum
Editorial Director: Ralph Graves
Group Vice President, Books: Joan D. Manley

TIME-LIFE BOOKS INC.

Editor: George Constable
Executive Editor: George Daniels
Director of Design: Louis Klein
Board of Editors: Dale M. Brown, Thomas A. Lewis,
Martin Mann, Robert G. Mason, Ellen Phillips,
Gerry Schremp, Gerald Simons, Rosalind Stubenberg,
Kit van Tulleken
Director of Administration: David L. Harrison
Director of Research: Carolyn L. Sackett
Director of Photography: John Conrad Weiser

President: Reginald K. Brack Jr.
Executive Vice President: John Steven Maxwell
Vice Presidents: George Artandi, Stephen L. Bair,
Peter G. Barnes, Nicholas Benton, John L. Canova,
Beatrice T. Dobie, Christopher T. Linen,
James L. Mercer, Paul R. Stewart

WORLD WAR II

Prisoners of War was prepared under the supervision
of Time-Life Books by the following contributors:
Editors: Charles Osborne, Sheldon Cotler
Picture Editor: Peter D. Collins
Assistant Designer: Leonard Vigliarolo
Researchers: Martha J. Mader, Suzanne Odette Khuri,
Starr Badger Shippee, Ronald J. Fagan,
John E. Taktikos, Marian H. Mundy
Writers: Rafael Steinberg, Cathy Beason,
Tony Chiu, R. H. Cravens, Don Earnest, Cinda Siler,
Bryce S. Walker
Art Assistant: Diana Raquel Vazquez
Editorial Manager: Felice Lerner
Editorial Assistants: Stacy Aronowitz,
Nicholas Goodman

Time-Life Books Editorial Staff for *Prisoners of War*
Researchers: Loretta Britten, Philip Brandt George
Copy Coordinators: Ann Bartunek, Allan Fallow,
Barbara F. Quarmby
Art Assistant: Robert K. Herndon
Picture Coordinator: Betty Hughes Weatherley
Editorial Assistant: Connie Strawbridge

Editorial Operations
Design: Arnold C. Holeywell (assistant director);
Anne B. Landry (art coordinator); James J. Cox
(quality control)
Research: Jane Edwin (assistant director),
Louise D. Forstall
Copy Room: Susan Galloway Goldberg (director),
Celia Beattie
Production: Feliciano Madrid (director),
Gordon E. Buck, Peter Inchauteguiz

Correspondents: Elisabeth Kraemer (Bonn); Margot
Hapgood, Dorothy Bacon, Lesley Coleman (London);
Susan Jonas, Lucy T. Voulgaris (New York); Maria
Vincenza Aloisi, Josephine du Brusle (Paris); Ann
Natanson (Rome). Valuable assistance was also
provided by Wibo Van de Linde, Bert Meijer
(Amsterdam); Robert Gilmore (Auckland); Helga Kohl
(Bonn); Judy Aspinall, Sylvia Pile (London); Trini
Bandrés (Madrid); John Dunn (Melbourne); Bruce
Nelan (Moscow); Carolyn Chubet, Miriam Hsia,
Christina Lieberman (New York); M. T. Hirschkoff
(Paris); Ernie Shirley (Queensland); Mimi Murphy
(Rome); Akio Fujii, Kazuo Ohyauchi (Tokyo).

The Author: RONALD H. BAILEY is a freelance author
and journalist. He is the author of *Violence and Ag-
gression* and *The Role of the Brain* in Time-Life Books
Human Behavior series, and of *The Home Front:
U.S.A., Partisans and Guerrillas,* and *The Air War in
Europe* in the World War II series. He has also published several articles on prison reform in *Corrections*
magazine; while a senior editor at *Life,* he edited a
book of Larry Burrows' war photographs, *Larry Burrows: Compassionate Photographer.*

The Consultants: COLONEL JOHN R. ELTING, USA (Ret.),
was an intelligence officer with the 8th Armored Division in World War II. A former associate professor at
West Point, he is the author of *Battles for Scandinavia*
in the Time-Life Books World War II series and of *The
Battle of Bunker's Hill, The Battles of Saratoga* and
Military History and Atlas of the Napoleonic Wars.

BROOKS KLEBER is Deputy Chief Historian of the U.S.
Army Center of Military History, and is a retired Army
Reserve colonel. An infantry commander in Normandy in June 1944, he was captured while on a recon-
naisance patrol. Following a stint of 10 months in
various German prison camps—he once spent five
days in solitary confinement—Kleber was liberated
by troops of General George S. Patton's Third Army in
April of 1945.

Library of Congress Cataloguing in Publication Data

Bailey, Ronald H.   1934-
    Prisoners of War

    (World War II; v. 30)
    Bibliography: p.
    Includes index.
        1. World War, 1939-1945—Prisoners and prisons.
    2. Prisoners of war—History—20th century.
    I. Time-Life Books.   II. Title.   III. Series.
    D805.A2B34   940.54'72   81-9403
                                AACR2
    ISBN 0-8094-3393-1
    ISBN 0-8094-3392-3 (lib. bdg.)
    ISBN 0-8094-3391-5 (retail ed.)

For information about any Time-Life book, please write:

Reader Information
Time-Life Books
541 North Fairbanks Court
Chicago, Illinois 60611

CONTENTS

THE FACES OF CAPTIVITY

BRITISH COMMONWEALTH, 1940

JAPANESE, 1945

AMERICAN, 1945

GERMAN, 1944

RUSSIAN, 1941

GERMAN, 1944

RUSSIAN, 1942

ITALIAN, 1943

7

1

THE WAR BEHIND THE WIRE

The War had not gone at all badly for Captain Julius M. Green, a young British dental officer. Late in the winter of 1939-1940, not long after the German invasion of Poland and the outbreak of war in Europe, Green had been sent to France to serve with an ambulance unit of the 51st Highland Division. And though his division had been hard pressed by the lightning advance of the German Army, he was enjoying himself. "The War had been a nice change from standing behind a dental chair practically all day, six days a week," he wrote later. "It had been interesting, exciting and in parts good fun."

Then on June 12, 1940, Green's ambulance unit found itself pinned against the English Channel at Saint Valéry, assaulted on three sides by the Germans and awaiting an evacuation by sea that never came. On that day word was passed down that the 51st Highlanders had formally surrendered. Green left his aid station and wandered through the streets of Saint Valéry to look for wounded comrades.

"As I turned a corner I saw a tank, its gun pointing in my direction. The hatch opened and a character in dungarees emerged holding an automatic, which he pointed at me."

"For you the War is over!" said the German.

That refrain—in German, *"Für Sie ist der Krieg vorbei!"*—was sounded on the battlefields of World War II in a dozen different tongues: in the "Milwaukee Deutsch," or pidgin German of American GIs; in Russian and Japanese, and in the universal language of a rifle butt to the ribs. It was heard, felt, endured by the estimated 15 million men and the handful of women who became prisoners of war.

For them, one war was over, but another was just beginning. This new war—the war behind barbed wire—was often no less dangerous than combat. Waged against disease, hunger, brutality, boredom and despair, it was a battle for survival that had to be fought without the benefit of the weapons or logistics that support modern armies. Moreover, it was conducted against a fully armed enemy captor who did what he could to use the prisoners' labor and to extract whatever military information they had. "You are in the power of your enemy," wrote Julius Green's countryman Prime Minister Winston Churchill, referring to his own experience as a war prisoner (he had been taken captive 41 years before as a correspondent covering the Boer War in South Africa). "You owe your life to his humanity, and your daily bread to his compassion. You must obey his orders, go where he tells you, stay where you are bid, await his pleasure, possess your soul in patience."

What Churchill called the "melancholy state" of a prisoner of war was not unique to the 20th Century. Since human beings first took up arms against one another, combatants had captured enemies. Never before, however, had so many prisoners of war been confined in so many places. Barbed-wire enclosures or their equivalents—electrified fences, bamboo stockades, barricades, walls of wood or stone—dotted the globe, from the United States and Canada through England, Italy, Germany and the Soviet Union, and into Asia, Australia, Japan and the islands of the Pacific.

In addition to the millions of military captives whom the combatants formally classified as prisoners of war, the vast stretches of barbed wire contained untold numbers of other people—perhaps as many as 20 million. These were civilians who, by reason of their nationality, race, religion or simply their availability for forced labor, were held against their will. Japan, for example, interned throughout the Pacific and in Asia more than 75,000 American, British, Dutch and other Allied civilians who, as missionaries, business people, diplomats, farmers or colonial administrators, happened to be in the wrong place when war came. Nazi Germany, to keep its war industries running, enslaved some five million laborers from Poland, France and other nations in occupied Europe. Germany also brought together in its infamous concentration camps, and then put to death, more than six million people, mostly Jews.

The risks of captivity in wartime had never been greater. Yet, for the first time in history, the treatment of military prisoners was governed—on paper, at least—by an extensive body of international rules embodied in the Geneva Convention. Named for the Swiss city where it was signed in July 1929 by 47 nations—including all World War II belligerents except the U.S.S.R.—the Convention was called by the Swiss government, working hand in hand with the International Committee of the Red Cross, a Swiss organization that is the umbrella for the world's 100-odd national Red Cross groups. The International Red Cross, devoted to the relief of all kinds of human suffering, had its beginnings in the plight of wounded men following the battle of Solferino, fought between the French and the Austrians in 1859.

A harrowing account of the wounded men's suffering, written by a Swiss named Jean Henri Dunant, attracted widespread attention in Europe. In 1864, representatives of 16 nations met in Switzerland, and 12 nations signed the first Geneva Convention, which established the Red Cross emblem (the reverse of the Swiss flag, a white cross on a red ground) and provided for the humane treatment of wounded in war—establishing, for example, the neutral status of military medical personnel.

In a similar spirit during World War I, neutral countries such as Switzerland took informal responsibility for the decent treatment of POWs—through measures that included inspections of camps and the hearing of prisoners' complaints out of earshot of their captors. Such protection got formal international recognition in the Geneva Convention of 1929, along with a number of other guiding principles. The Convention defined a prisoner of war as a uniform-wearing member of a regular military unit, a definition that excluded guerrillas, spies and other irregular warriors. The Convention dictated that a POW "must at all times be humanely treated" and spelled out in considerable detail the rights of the captive and the obligations of the captor. A prisoner's food, clothing and shelter, for example, were to be equal to that of the captor's own troops. He was to be allowed to communicate with his family. If not an officer he could be required to work, but only at jobs that did not jeopardize his health or relate directly to war operations.

In practice, application of the rules was unpredictable: How a prisoner fared behind wire depended less upon the humanitarian provisions of the Geneva Convention than upon the widely varying customs and attitudes of his captors—and on wartime conditions. Even when a nation generally adhered to the Convention, a prisoner's welfare might hinge upon the men who happened to be guarding him. American Private Harold J. Farrell recalled that when his fellow prisoners complained about being forced to work too many hours, their German guard tapped his rifle and said, "Here is my Geneva Convention."

The principal problem with the Geneva Convention was the fact that three major powers—Japan, the Soviet Union and Germany—ignored its provisions in varying degrees. Japan had signed the Convention in 1929 but announced soon af-

A WORLD OF MILITARY PRISONS

The global sweep of World War II was reflected in the way most of the 15 million prisoners of war were distributed. As shown in these maps, camps were established on three continents, on the islands of the United Kingdom and Japan, and in Japan's overseas possessions. Allied installations are indicated by blue dots, Axis camps by red dots. Each dot stands for one camp, except in the Far East, where each dot represents about three camps.

Japan held most of its POWs on the Asian mainland and in such wartime island acquisitions as the Dutch East Indies. The majority of German camps were in the Reich and in German-ruled western Poland. After 1943, Germans took over

Italy's camps, including those in Greece.

The distribution of the U.S.S.R.'s camps roughly followed that of the existing prison network, augmented by new camps in Soviet-controlled eastern Poland. Relatively few POW installations are shown on the map below; although the Soviet Union ran some 3,000 camps, only about 5 per cent of them can be documented accurately. Partly to take advantage of the prisoners' labor potential, the United States and Canada built many camps in agricultural areas. Most British camps were in England, with a scattering in Wales, Scotland and Northern Ireland. Everywhere, the number of camps and prisoners changed monthly with the progress of the War.

Between 1940 and 1945 Great Britain, the Soviet Union and the Berlin-Rome Axis maintained the camps shown above. British camps numbered 86; the

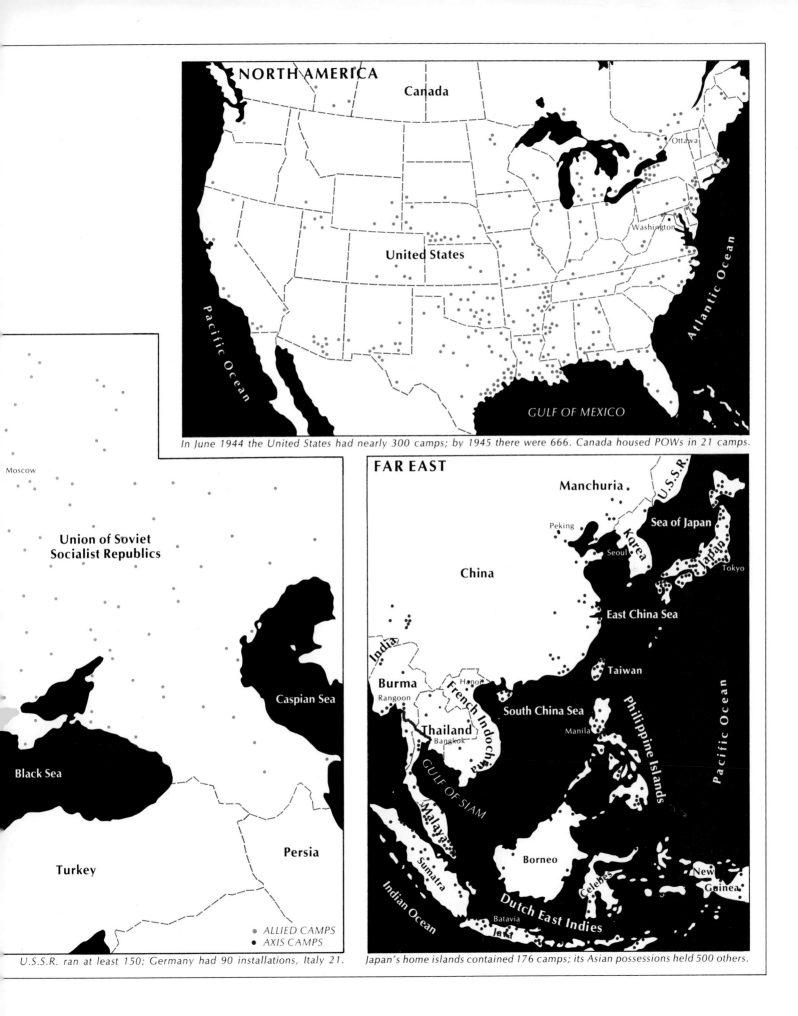

NORTH AMERICA

Canada

Ottawa

United States

Washington

Pacific Ocean

Atlantic Ocean

GULF OF MEXICO

In June 1944 the United States had nearly 300 camps; by 1945 there were 666. Canada housed POWs in 21 camps.

Moscow

**Union of Soviet
Socialist Republics**

Caspian Sea

Black Sea

Turkey

Persia

● *ALLIED CAMPS*
● *AXIS CAMPS*

U.S.S.R. ran at least 150; Germany had 90 installations, Italy 21.

FAR EAST

Manchuria

U.S.S.R.

Peking

Sea of Japan

Korea

Seoul

Japan

Tokyo

China

East China Sea

India

Taiwan

Burma

Hanoi

French Indochina

Rangoon

South China Sea

Thailand

Manila

Bangkok

GULF OF SIAM

Philippine Islands

Pacific Ocean

Malaya

Sumatra

Borneo

Celebes

New Guinea

Indian Ocean

Dutch East Indies

Batavia

Java

Japan's home islands contained 176 camps; its Asian possessions held 500 others.

ter attacking Pearl Harbor on December 7, 1941, that it would comply with the terms *mutatis mutandis*—a legalism meaning "necessary changes having been made." This turned out to mean hardly complying at all. The Soviet Union, which had been isolated from the international community during the 1920s, had not attended the meetings that produced the Geneva Convention and made no effort to follow its rules. Germany, for its part, took a contradictory stance, ignoring the Convention on the Eastern Front while generally abiding by it in handling prisoners from France, the United States and Britain on the Western Front.

The intransigence of both the Soviet Union and Japan stemmed largely from strongly held national and political attitudes about the status of their own fighting men as prisoners—attitudes that they projected upon the prisoners whom they themselves captured. The Soviet dictator, Josef Stalin, expected his soldiers to fight to the death; a Russian who fell into enemy hands, Stalin feared, might become converted to non-Marxist ideas. The Japanese attitude, on the other hand, derived from cultural tradition rather than ideology. A Japanese soldier's behavior on the battlefield was governed by ancient rules of conduct known as *Bushido*—the Way of the Warrior.

Bushido was above all a code of honor—and shame. The American anthropologist Ruth Benedict wrote in her postwar study of Japanese culture, *The Chrysanthemum and the Sword:* "Honor was bound up with fighting to the death. In a hopeless situation, a soldier should kill himself with his last hand grenade or charge weaponless against the enemy in a mass suicide attack. But he should not surrender."

The shame of surrender was burned so deeply into the Japanese conscience that, until the final months of the war in the Pacific, only a few thousand Japanese were taken prisoner by the Allies—and many of those lay wounded and helpless at the moment of capture. During the 1944-1945 campaign in Burma, 142 Japanese soldiers were captured whereas 17,166 were killed—a ratio of 1 to 120. Among the Western armies, by contrast, commanders expected an overall captured-to-killed ratio of only 1 to 4.

Perhaps the most extraordinary illustration of the Japanese attitude toward surrender and its consequence, captivity, was the case of Army Lieutenant Hiro Onoda. Trained in guerrilla tactics, Onoda was landed on Lubang in the north-ern Philippines early in 1945, the last year of the War, with instructions to help the island's weary garrison prevent capture of the airstrip by American invasion forces. The Americans seized the airstrip and captured or killed the rest of the Japanese soldiers. But Onoda, under orders to hold out until reinforcements arrived, fought on in the jungles of Lubang.

Though the War ended, nothing could persuade Onoda to surrender. Leaflets announcing the capitulation of Japan, newspapers and magazines air-dropped into the jungle, the voice of his brother over a loudspeaker—all of these, Onoda believed, were enemy tricks. Living off the land and sustaining his resolution by repeating to himself passages from the Japanese Military Field Code, which embodied the tenets of *Bushido,* Onoda held out for 30 years.

In 1975, a young Japanese named Norio Suzuki hit on a way to persuade Onoda to emerge from the jungle. Figuring that Onoda would be lonely, he pitched a tent as close to the veteran's hideout as he could, and waited for him to come out and talk. Onoda did approach, and Suzuki managed to convince the older man that the War had indeed

ended, and that it would be in keeping with military tradition—Suzuki quoted persuasively from the copy of the Japanese warrior's code that he had brought along—to give up. Onoda agreed to surrender, but only after receiving orders from his commanding officer—by then a bookseller in Kyoto—who was duly brought to Lubang, where he read him Emperor Hirohito's 1945 proclamation of surrender.

Because they made no concession to foreign attitudes in the matter, the Japanese abhorrence of surrender directly influenced their handling of prisoners from other nations. By allowing themselves to be taken captive, these men—in the Japanese view—merited only contempt. They were to be punished for their cowardice with starvation diets, brutally hard work and physical abuse. Largely as a result, more than 28 per cent of the 95,000 Britons, Americans, Canadians, Australians and New Zealanders taken prisoner by the Japanese died in captivity. By contrast, only 4 per cent died among the 260,000 British and American prisoners captured by the Germans.

The Russians, following the pattern set by Stalin (who

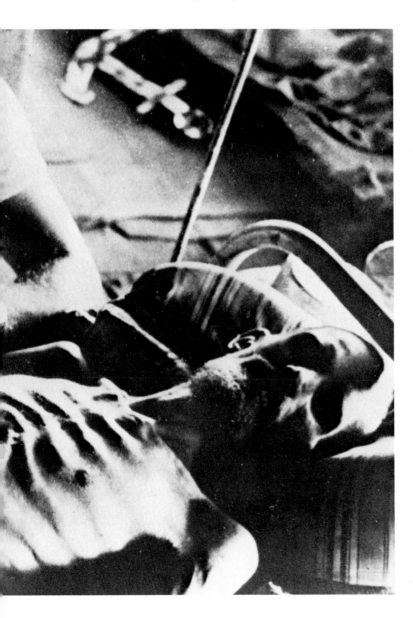

wrote off his own POWs) and imbued with a traditional hatred for Germans, tended to deny the humanity of those they captured. In practical terms, this shrank the odds for the survival of a German prisoner to little better than 50-50. On the German side, Nazi racial theories equating Russians and other Slavs with animals doomed such POWs to lives of unrelieved desperation.

Whatever the policies of their captors, the reaction of the prisoners to captivity varied widely. With the exception of the Japanese, few fighting men faced surrender with feelings of shame or dishonor. The mechanization of modern warfare, with its quick armored thrusts, had made it inevitable that large numbers of men would be captured. Instead of shame, the newly taken prisoner might feel shock; or he might experience uncertainty, relief at no longer being shot at, or indignation at the conduct of his captors.

German Sergeant Reinhold Pabel, who was wounded in the chest before being captured by the Americans in 1943 at the Volturno River in Italy, remembered his "first bitter taste of being a prisoner." He was carried to a POW collecting station and "as soon as the stretcher had been placed on the floor, a bunch of souvenir hunters ripped some of my decorations off my blouse. After they had done so they asked me if I had any objections. I kept my mouth shut."

A prisoner's first few hours in captivity were often the worst. Airmen in particular were likely to encounter hostility when they were shot down over enemy-held territory. People on the ground were eager to get their hands on the men who had been bombing or strafing them. In Germany, which suffered heavy Allied bombing attacks late in the War, mobs of civilians sometimes attempted to lynch downed airmen.

One of the most brutal such assaults occurred on August 26, 1944, when eight members of a U.S. bomber crew were shot down and captured near Hanover in northern Germany. Guarded by two German soldiers, the airmen boarded a train to a POW camp near Frankfurt am Main. When the train reached the outskirts of the small town of Rüsselsheim, however, it was forced to halt because of bomb damage to the tracks. The guards then set out to march their eight captives through the streets to a train on the other side of town.

Suddenly a mob of German civilians, including two

A photograph taken in June of 1943 with a homemade camera using X-ray film shows prisoner-medics attempting to treat an emaciated American POW at the Japanese camp at Cabanatuan, in the Philippine Islands. Most of the 10,000 prisoners there suffered from multiple diseases, including dysentery, beriberi, malaria, scurvy and pellagra—all of which were aggravated, if not actually caused, by slow starvation. One quarter of the prisoners died in the first eight months of captivity.

13

women, set upon the Americans with cries of "Beat them to death!" The mob pelted the prisoners with stones and struck them with clubs, shovels, hammers and large chunks of roof tile. As the Americans struggled forward, their assailants were urged on by Joseph Hartgen, a local Nazi official. Finally, after two hours of beatings, the Americans collapsed just as they neared the safety of the waiting train. Hartgen then pulled his pistol and pumped bullets into the fallen airmen. Someone borrowed a cart from a nearby farm, and their assailants hauled the Americans off to the town cemetery to be buried the following day.

Six of them were buried. But two of the Americans, though badly hurt, managed to escape from the cart during the night. After several days of hiding, they were picked up by a German patrol and sent to a POW camp. To spare the families of the murder victims, the two men pledged each other to silence. They broke their vows only after the War, when they were witnesses at a widely publicized trial by a U.S. military tribunal, which sentenced seven of their civilian assailants, including Joseph Hartgen, to death.

No one knows how many prisoners were summarily executed by civilians or soldiers in the first hours and days after surrender. Germany, by the testimony of its own official records, killed no fewer than 473,000 Russian POWs during the War—many of them soon after capture. Some Germans and Japanese responsible for summary executions of Allied captives were tried and punished after the War. But battlefield crimes against prisoners by the War's victors generally went unpublicized and unpunished.

Most prisoners who survived the first few days of captivity faced a long journey by foot, truck, train or ship: The typical POW generally traveled from a temporary detention area near the battlefield or other place of capture to a permanent camp, usually in the captor's homeland.

The circumstances of the journey to the permanent camp varied widely. German prisoners were borne from the battlefields of North Africa, Italy and Western Europe to camps in the United States on uncrowded transports where many slept in cabins. On the other hand, American, Dutch, British and Commonwealth troops captured in the Pacific and Southeast Asia were crammed into the airless holds of freighters for the trip to the Japanese homeland. Lieutenant John F. Kinney, an American pilot, recalled that the heroic defenders of Wake Island were hauled aboard ship in cargo nets, then made to run a gantlet of Japanese sailors, who beat them with rifle butts, clubs and sheathed swords. Such Japanese ships seldom bore Red Cross markings to indicate they were carrying prisoners of war. As a result, thousands of POWs died when the ships came under attack by Allied planes or submarines.

The journey to permanent camps could be complicated by the combined effect of the captives' debilities and the captors' wartime priorities. Newly taken prisoners, already weakened by hunger or disease, got even hungrier and sicker when their captors—pressed by the logistic needs of their own forces—were unprepared to transport or feed large numbers of men.

Such was the case in the most infamous of the so-called death marches—the trek undertaken by the American and Filipino defenders of Bataan after their surrender on April 9, 1942. Lacking sufficient transport, the Japanese forced some 78,000 captives, many ill or wounded, to march more than 65 miles north from Bataan to Camp O'Donnell. About 650 Americans and between 5,000 and 10,000 Filipinos died during the march—many of them clubbed, bayoneted or shot to death by Japanese guards. Those who made it to Camp O'Donnell, said an American doctor who survived the march, did so "on the marrow of their bones."

On the Eastern Front in Europe, the journey was even more arduous. There, trains were used to carry POWs the vast distances between battlefields and permanent camps in either Germany or the Soviet Union. Prisoners were stuffed into cattle cars, with little food or medical attention and no heat in winter. When one trainload of Germans captured in western Russia arrived at a camp at Yelabuga on the Volga River, it held 700 frozen corpses—victims of typhus, typhoid, dysentery and bitter cold. Russians who made the trip in the other direction, to camps in Germany, sometimes jumped off the trains en route—not so much to escape, it was said, as to die with some dignity in the open air rather than in the horror and stench of the cars.

For all its hardships, the trip to a permanent camp often afforded the best opportunities for a prisoner to escape and regain his freedom. During the War, the number of Royal Air Force prisoners of war who eluded their guards en route

RETRIEVING HONOR THROUGH DEATH

Shortly before 2 a.m. on a moonlit night in August of 1944 a bugle sounded at a POW camp in Cowra, Australia. Within seconds more than 1,000 Japanese prisoners surged toward the barbed-wire fence, shouting "Banzai!" their traditional battle cry. They brandished nail-studded baseball bats, kitchen knives and other crude weapons. The prisoners were met with gunfire from the Australian guards, but the bullets failed to stop them. Wave after wave of frenzied prisoners assaulted the fence, clambering over the bodies of dead and dying comrades caught high on the wire, only to be mowed down themselves.

Two hundred and thirty-one prisoners died and another 107 were injured in the uprising. Some 334 did get out of the camp, but their Oriental faces were conspicuous and all were either picked up or killed within days.

The Japanese leaders had an ostensible military objective for the assault: to take over the camp and, using captured arms, attack a nearby infantry training center. But most of the men, including their leaders, believed the scheme to be futile—suicidal, in fact. In the planning phase, one proponent of the attempt confirmed his motive, asserting: "It is a chance to die."

That was the prisoners' real goal: Only by dying could they fulfill the obligations of *Bushido*—an ancient Japanese code of conduct that equates surrender with dishonor. The Japanese suffered deep shame over their captivity and constantly brooded about redeeming their dignity in death.

All joined in the decision to attack. During the quiet hours before H-hour, the men prepared themselves for death—writing poems, cutting locks of hair to be sent home to families, taking leave of friends. Before the assault was launched, those too infirm to take part took their own lives inside the barracks.

In the aftermath, those who survived were disconsolate. One unhappy survivor, expressing his hope for another chance to die, declared: "We will show them the essence of *Bushido;* we are Japanese."

Instigator of a suicidal breakout from a prisoner-of-war camp in Australia, Sergeant Major Masao Kojima hangs from a noose he rigged in the compound kitchen.

to a permanent German camp and then got home to England was four times greater than the number of British airmen who successfully escaped from permanent camps.

For many prisoners, the journey to a permanent camp was punctuated by intensive sessions of interrogation by their captors. New prisoners were a prime source of information; soon after surrendering, they were usually questioned briefly about the strength and disposition of their units and searched for maps, letters from home or diaries—any documents that might provide clues. In the case of an airman, even a seemingly innocuous item such as a movie-theater ticket stub might point to the location of his home base. Such searches and questioning were permitted under the Geneva Convention, but in answering a prisoner was required to divulge only his name, rank and service number.

Before being sent to a permanent camp, certain prisoners—especially airmen, submarine crews and high-ranking officers—were taken to special interrogation centers that were common to the POW processing systems of all the major powers. There, trained interrogators sought data about weapons and units, and the enemy's economy and morale.

In this endeavor, the interrogator might employ a variety of methods, ranging from psychological subterfuge to physical violence. Representatives of every major power probably resorted to physical abuse at one time or another; the Japanese, in particular, were notorious for cruelty during questioning. At Ofuna, near Yokohama, the Japanese maintained an interrogation center for captured Allied submarine crews where the techniques were so brutal—beating, bayoneting, forcing bamboo splinters under the fingernails—that it was known to American and British prisoners as Torture Farm. But physical methods seldom paid off. Though the Japanese, for example, badly wanted to learn the maximum diving depth of U.S. submarines and probably used torture in their attempts to get the information, these specifications remained among the War's best-kept secrets.

More sophisticated and more effective was the form of interrogation used by the British from the beginning of the War. German prisoners arriving in England were put in one of nine centers known as Cages. They were first questioned by sergeants from British Army Intelligence, most of whom were German-Jewish refugees who, of course, spoke perfect German. These sergeants obtained such essential details as the prisoner's hometown and civilian job and nominated for further questioning the men—approximately 1 in 10—whom they suspected of having valuable information.

The interrogation officers relied on what one British Cage chief called "processes of painless extraction." The officer, who usually knew a great deal about Nazi Germany—often from time spent there before the War as a student or businessman—would engage the prisoner in friendly conversation about general subjects, then subtly guide the conversation to matters of military importance. To encourage talk, officers at the Cage at Wilton Park near London would take their subjects for walks in the nearby woods. The officer might remark upon the aircraft flying overhead and then, casually, elicit technical details about German planes without the prisoner's realizing he was giving away useful information. To keep these woodland walks from becoming invitations to escape, there was a security system: The trees were wired at intervals on the path with electrical connections to the orderly room. At successive checkpoints the officer would push a button affixed to a tree so that the orderly would know his precise whereabouts.

Sometimes the subject of an interrogation was lodged in a cell with another German prisoner and their conversations were picked up by a hidden microphone. A Luftwaffe pilot quickly spotted a microphone rather obviously hidden in a ventilator grill; but when he and his companion leaned out the window to talk away from the electronic intruder, the pilot realized another microphone had been secreted in the window frame. On more than one occasion the fellow prisoner was not a German at all, but a British officer so well-informed about his companion's background that he could successfully pretend to be practically a next-door neighbor.

Most of the particulars of what the British were able to learn by such techniques are still shrouded in official secrecy. But it is known that two captured German generals let drop the first hints of a vitally important secret: that the V-2 rocket was being prepared at the Peenemünde missile test center in the Baltic Sea. This intelligence, along with other information about the rocket program, led to the decision to bomb Peenemünde on the night of August 17, 1943.

Such British interrogation methods made a lasting impression on one of the German prisoners. Lieutenant Franz von

Werra, a young fighter ace who was shot down over England in 1940, found that his interrogator seemed to know everything about him, even the fact that the pilot had a pet lion cub. (The interrogator had seen Werra's picture with the cub in a German magazine.) After questioning and a period of confinement in England, Werra was shipped to Canada. There he escaped from a train in January 1941 and made his way over the border into the United States, which was not yet at war. With the help of German diplomats he finally got back to Germany, where he persuaded Air Force chief Hermann Göring to remodel the Luftwaffe's own interrogation center along British lines.

The Luftwaffe interrogation center was at Oberursel, seven miles northwest of Frankfurt. Nearby was Dulag Luft, the transit camp where captured British and American airmen were taken before being assigned to permanent camps. After Werra's successful intervention with Göring, Allied airmen met an increasingly sophisticated system of questioning at Oberursel, which by 1944 had a staff of 300 and was equipped to process 2,000 airmen a month.

The Germans took the British techniques and added some special twists of their own. After arriving at Oberursel the prisoner was put in solitary confinement, but fairly soon he found himself being greeted by a friendly, English-speaking interrogator. After chatting pleasantly for a few minutes, the interrogator would ask the prisoner to fill out what he described as a Red Cross questionnaire. As Lieutenant Ken-

neth Simmons, a B-24 bombardier from Texas, remembered it, the form had 50 questions. It began innocently enough with blanks for name, rank and service number, but went on to ask increasingly pointed questions, ending with the request to describe the strength of Allied air forces in Europe. Simmons, who had been warned about the form at his base in England, simply crossed out the final 47 questions. Meanwhile, however, his interrogator was assessing his personality and developing recommendations for the approach to be used during full-scale interrogation a few days later.

One of the most skilled interrogators at Oberursel was Hanns Scharff, who, though only a corporal, had charge of questioning most U.S. fighter pilots. Scharff spoke excellent English; before the War he had spent 10 years as a businessman in South Africa and England. He had a genuine admiration for the exploits of American fighter aces. And he never missed the *Terry and the Pirates* comic strip—featuring American fliers—published in *Stars and Stripes,* the daily newspaper for U.S. servicemen, which Scharff obtained through neutral Portugal.

Like other Luftwaffe interrogators, Scharff sometimes resorted to an underhanded gambit, insisting that his subject prove that he was indeed an American airman and not a spy. After all, he would suggest in a confidential tone, spies had to be turned over to the Gestapo. This trick usually got the prisoner to protest—and start talking about himself.

Scharff never approached the interrogation process head on. The heart of his indirect technique was small talk, fueled by inside information. When he questioned a new prisoner, he had before him a dossier on the man and his unit compiled from a number of sources. Oberursel maintained extensive files of clippings from American and British newspapers, as well as reports from German agents in England. Scharff even had available transcripts of the radio conversations of Allied pilots, which were monitored by Luftwaffe ground stations. By 1944, the files of Scharff and the other interrogators at Oberursel were bulging.

Thus prepared, Scharff could often overwhelm a prisoner with intimate knowledge, giving him the impression that divulging a few more details would not be harmful. Alternatively, Scharff would extract seemingly unrelated bits of information from one interrogation and fit them together into a mosaic that would prove valuable in questioning other

One of the Luftwaffe's most adept interrogators was Hanns Scharff, whose command of the English language earned him a transfer in 1943 from a tank outfit—about to be dispatched to the Russian front—to a headquarters unit and eventually into Air Force intelligence work.

prisoners. Colonel Hubert Zemke, who was questioned by Scharff after being forced down in October 1944, was astounded by the man's ability to wring information from reluctant airmen with the leverage of idle chatter. "I had the impression," Zemke said later, "that it might even be dangerous just to talk about the weather with him."

If a prisoner talked, even about the weather, he was rewarded, perhaps with a pleasant dinner accompanied by wine. Prisoners who remained silent were sent back to solitary, where it was a common practice of the German guards to manipulate the temperature so that the cell, as a British airman described it, was alternately "cooled below freezing point and then brought up to an unbreathable Turkish bath heat." The resulting discomfort was deemed to be eloquently persuasive with recalcitrants, though there is no way of proving whether it was effective or not. After a few days or a week at Oberursel, most prisoners were sent on to a permanent camp, but some were subjected to such carrot-and-stick methods for up to a month.

Scharff, in his memoir, *The Interrogator,* is vague as to the military significance of much of what he learned. Clearly, however, he greatly enjoyed his job and seems to have made friends with a number of his subjects. He took them to church and to parties, and got them to inscribe personal messages in a guestbook of sorts. Once, he even arranged for an American colonel to visit a Luftwaffe base, where the American was allowed to take off alone for a spin in an Me-109 fighter. (The ground crew had first made sure that there was not enough gasoline in the plane for the prisoner to make it back to England.) Scharff was so friendly to his subjects, in fact, that he was more than once reprimanded by his superiors for fraternizing with the prisoners.

While a prisoner was undergoing questioning at Oberursel or any of the other interrogation centers maintained by the major warring nations, he was also being scrutinized as a potential collaborator. The interrogator looked for motives for collaboration on the prisoner's part—sympathy with his captor's political ideology, perhaps, or simply the desire to avoid the hardships of a POW camp. Prisoners of all nationalities collaborated during the War, though in numbers and in ways that varied greatly from one country to another.

A common kind of collaboration was eavesdropping by cooperative prisoners planted in camps to pick up information. Such stool pigeons might obtain data of military significance or news of an impending escape attempt. They ran the risk of discovery by their fellow prisoners, of course; exposure brought swift prison justice, ranging from social ostracism to a sound thrashing and sometimes death.

Another use of collaborators was in the psychological warfare waged against their countrymen in the combat zones. Prisoners were recruited to write propaganda leaflets and to broadcast over radios and loudspeakers in the front lines, appealing to their comrades to surrender. In Burma, a group from the U.S. Office of War Information succeeded in organizing a six-man propaganda team of Japanese POWs in the summer of 1944. The team prepared scripts for front-line broadcasts and wrote leaflets to be air-dropped. Ironically, the intermediaries who were able to crack the prisoners' code of honor were nisei—Japanese-American—interpreters, whose own families had been interned in the United States after the attack on Pearl Harbor.

Collaborators also served as leaders—managing, training and teaching in programs aimed at changing the political attitudes of their fellow prisoners. Late in the War, for example, the Americans and British undertook a large-scale "re-education" of German POWs, hoping to prevent a renaissance of Nazism in postwar Germany. Their methods were largely intellectual, using classroom lessons in democracy. The Soviet Union took quite a different approach: With a view toward creating friendly Communists to dominate Eastern Europe after the War, the Soviets extended to enemy prisoners the methods they had already perfected on their own citzens during the 1930s. These methods, combining physical and psychological violence and known as "brainwashing," aimed at nothing less than altering the very character and personality of the prisoner.

In some cases, collaborators were actually induced to take up arms against their own nation or its allies. Beginning in 1943, Germany mounted a campaign for British prisoners to join an outfit known at first as the Legion of Saint George and later as the British Free Corps. The propaganda played upon the fear of Communism, and the legion's ostensible purpose was to fight the Soviet Union. The legion was the brainchild of John Amery, a civilian who was the son of a respected former British Cabinet member. Young Amery, a

WOMEN: SEPARATE BUT EQUAL TREATMENT

Among the thousands of American troops captured on Corregidor in May 1942 were 67 U.S. Army and Navy nurses who spent the next 33 months in captivity with Allied and American civilians. Though the women were spared the brutal physical abuse that was meted out to male prisoners, they too subsisted on a starvation diet of rice, greens and gruel, and suffered from diseases. Miraculously, all of the nurses lived to be liberated.

Nurses, because they were members of the armed forces, were subject to imprisonment as POWs. Germany had nearly 500,000 women in uniform as support troops, and Russian women not only carried rifles but served their country as combat pilots as well.

German and Russian women were not as fortunate as the American nurses. They were segregated from the men, but they did the same work and suffered desperate privations. There were an estimated 25,000 to 30,000 German women prisoners of war; how many Russian women soldiers passed through or perished in camps is unknown. Once they were captured, the Russian women were sent to forced-labor camps with their civilian counterparts, and their numbers only added to the millions of Russian citizens who disappeared while in the hands of the Third Reich.

American nurses and male hospital staffers on Corregidor were photographed by a Japanese newsman after the island fell in May 1942.

womanizer and a heavy drinker with an obsessive hatred of Communism, had left England at the age of 24 in 1937 to join the profascist forces of Franco during the Spanish Civil War. In 1942 Amery went to Berlin, where—like his better-known countryman, William Joyce ("Lord Haw-Haw")—he broadcast propaganda to his homeland.

In early 1943, encouraged by the Nazis to recruit prisoners for the legion, Amery toured camps in Germany where British were held and selected some prospects. Meanwhile, the Germans set up two so-called holiday camps to which selected British prisoners were sent for a month of "rest." Guests were given ample food and entertained with concerts, operas and motion pictures. The program was flavored with a bit of German propaganda, designed to convert the British to the Nazi cause.

British POWs enjoyed their holidays, but as recruiting centers the camps proved to be failures. In all, only 30-odd prisoners volunteered for service with Germany. Most were attracted not by Nazi ideology or by the fear of Communism, but by the lure of unlimited supplies of liquor and the availability of German prostitutes. These recruits did a little military drill, learned German and, as one of them later put it, "otherwise did nothing except lay around, and go into the town, where we drank and associated with women."

The British Free Corps never did see combat against the Russians or anyone else. Its principal function, British author Rebecca West pointed out in her book, *The New Meaning of Treason,* was to serve as a kind of reverse propaganda, aimed at the German people. Its role was to make the British look weak and incapable. As she described it, the Nazis dressed the Free Corps members "in German uniforms with flashes with the letters B.F.C. and the Union Jack to show that the wearers were British soldiers, and let them go rotten with idleness and indiscipline and debauchery. . . . There were never many of them. But even so small a number, split into groups and sent into the German towns, drunken and with prostitutes on their arms, did something to raise national morale in 1944 and 1945 and persuade the Germans that it was all true, what they had been told, and that they could not possibly be conquered by those degenerate people the British."

Not least of the reasons for the failure of the Free Corps was Sergeant John Brown, a British secret agent. Before the War, Brown had infiltrated the home-grown fascist movement of Sir Oswald Mosley on behalf of British intelligence. When war broke out, Brown turned to combating treachery in the British Army. Taken prisoner in France in 1940, he set out to win the confidence of the Germans, and eventually he was put in charge of the holiday camp for British enlisted men in Genshagen, near Berlin. This was a handy cover for Brown's work of subverting the Free Corps and gathering evidence against British traitors—including Lord Haw-Haw, who frequently used Free Corps members on his broadcasts. Through coded letters, Brown kept British intelligence apprised of his activities. After the War he was the chief prosecution witness at 20 treason trials, including the trials of Lord Haw-Haw and John Amery and a dozen or so of their followers.

In light of their ill-fated attempts to recruit British POWs, it is noteworthy that, with little effort, the Germans were able to raise an army of several hundred thousand Russian prisoners to fight against Stalin. Many of the turncoats were driven by political motives; they hated Stalin and wanted to rid their homeland of Communism. But others joined the German cause just to survive. So brutal was the German treatment of Russian POWs that anything, even treason, seemed preferable to prison camp.

A prisoner who survived the moment of capture, the ordeal of interrogation, the enemy's attempts to subvert him and the exigencies of wartime travel finally settled into a POW camp. His accommodations might consist of anything from a flimsy bamboo hut in the jungles of Southeast Asia to a solid wooden barracks in Texas. His residence in the camp might last for years or months. Depending on demands for prisoner labor or the view the authorities took of a group's propensity for escape or troublemaking, POWs were often moved from one camp to another.

In adjusting to his new home, a prisoner's primary concern usually focused on essentials—above all else, getting enough to eat. The problem varied in intensity: A prisoner in the hands of the United States or Britain ate better than he would have at home; a Russian in a German camp or an Allied POW in Japanese hands often had to struggle by on a starvation diet of as little as 500 to 600 calories a day. The rations of the typical Allied prisoner in German or Italian camps fell somewhere between these extremes—perhaps 1,500 calories a day; though hardly enough, this ration was supplemented by parcels of food sanctioned by the Geneva Convention and distributed under the auspices of the International Red Cross.

A Red Cross food parcel was 10 inches square, 4½ inches deep, weighed precisely 11 pounds (to conform with German postal regulations) and was the prisoner's most precious possession. It contained such staples as dried fruits, canned meat and fish, crackers, cheese, margarine, dried milk and such extras as jam, chocolate, cigarettes and soap. Each American and British prisoner in Europe was to receive one parcel a week; because procuring supplies was more difficult for governments-in-exile, such as those of France and Poland, their POWs received monthly parcels. In addition, each prisoner in Germany was allowed to receive a parcel from his family every two months.

Food parcels for all Allied POWs were prepared by the British Red Cross and the American Red Cross and were largely financed by the U.S. and British goverments. Agen-

cies such as the American YMCA also put together periodic shipments of recreational material such as sports equipment and books. The Red Cross, using government-issue uniform materials from the home authorities and garments knitted and sewed by volunteers, furnished clothing and medical supplies ranging from aspirin to blood plasma. Packages bound for camps in Germany and Italy went by ship, usually to Lisbon in neutral Portugal, and eventually by train to Geneva warehouses to await distribution by rail and truck by the International Red Cross.

The American Red Cross, which handled POW relief for all of the Western Allies except Great Britain, sent nearly 200,000 tons of food, clothing and medicines—so many parcels, it was said, that laid end to end they would have reached from Chicago to Berlin.

In other parts of the world, however, Red Cross parcels scarcely existed. The Soviet Union refused to participate in the relief activities of the International Red Cross; the tragic result was that Germans in Soviet hands received no parcels and, in retaliation, Russians in German hands got none ei-

ther. Japan justified its noncooperation on military grounds, barring relief ships from entering the waters it controlled. Consequently, only a thin stream of supplies from the American and British Red Cross trickled through to POWs in the Far East. Infrequent and scarce, these arrived through indirect channels—for example, from neutral-flag relief-agency ships meeting Japanese vessels in out-of-the-way ports such as Lourenço Marques in Portuguese Mozambique. The parcels that made it through to the camps were often pilfered and consumed by Japanese guards and other authorities. Rare was the Allied prisoner in the Far East who received more than one parcel a year.

Physical survival was only the beginning of the battle behind barbed wire. There remained a mental and emotional struggle. Probably every prisoner at one time or another was assaulted by the destructive emotions of captivity: extreme irritability at being confined with too many others in too little space; outrage at the injustice of being locked up for no apparent crime; the loneliness of being cut off from home and loved ones year after year. POWs who succumbed to such feelings often became so despondent that, in the vernacular of the prison camps, they went "wire-happy." Among such prisoners, suicide was common.

For all POWs, the consolations were few—and their benefits were mixed. Mail, the prisoner's one continuing link with home, was both a blessing and a bane. Many prisoners cracked under the strain of waiting for months or even years to hear from their loved ones.

No mail at all reached some camps. Germany and the Soviet Union made no provisions for the delivery of letters to their respective prisoners. Even when allowed, the writing and sending of letters could be complicated. In Japanese-run camps, prisoners had to use preprinted forms on which they were permitted to fill in only a few words. Apparently on the same principle of enforcing brevity, the Japanese limited incoming letters to 25 words, and these messages had to negotiate a tortuous route eastward arranged by neutral diplomats: from Allied post offices to Egypt, from there to Iran, by Soviet diplomatic pouch to Moscow, then by the Trans-Siberian Railroad to the border of Japanese-held territory in Manchuria. The wife of General Jonathan Wainwright, commander of American troops in the Philippines when Corregidor fell in May of 1942, wrote to her husband more than 300 times; six letters reached him.

Though Allied prisoners in Europe got letters much more frequently, the news was not always good. Every camp had its share of letters of rejection from wives and sweethearts who could not tolerate the long separation and became involved with other men. Thousands of these unlucky prisoners obtained divorces through the International Red Cross, which set up an office in Geneva to handle the paperwork.

To the Americans, in prison and out, such letters were "Dear Johns." To men of the Royal Air Force they were "Mespots"—for Mesopotamia, the Middle East area between the Tigris and Euphrates Rivers in what is now Iraq. The area had been controlled by Britain between the World Wars, and RAF personnel stationed there before World War II did five-year tours of duty without leave; marital breakup was a frequent result.

Since a Mespot was sometimes enough to drive the recipient wire-happy, British prisoners of war in many camps adopted another custom from the days in Mesopotamia. They pinned the letter on the camp bulletin board—in effect, publishing it. This served as a kind of group therapy, enabling others to share the grief of the rejected prisoner with him and help ease his feelings of loneliness. Some of the Mespot letters were gems. A concise five-word message sent to a British sergeant at Lamsdorf, Germany, by his best girl had everyone in camp laughing: "Sorry. Married your father. Mother."

In the fight to stay whole and sane, probably the greatest threat to a prisoner was the unremitting tedium of camp life. Even if he worked—almost all enlisted men did, and so did some officers—he was still confronted with endless empty hours. To fill the void, POWs staged theatrical productions and concerts, turned out camp newspapers, even set up "barbed-wire universities" where prisoners could gain college credit. Americans in Germany played baseball with equipment provided by the YMCA; Germans in the Soviet Union played soccer with balls improvised from discarded truck inner tubes.

Necessity mothered activities that sustained both body and soul. In Singapore, where more than 50,000 Australian and British soldiers were penned in a 12-square-mile area called Changi on the northeast tip of the island, the Japa-

GOOD NEWS FROM "DAD'S" LISTENING POST: "I'M ALL RIGHT!"

James and Mary MacMannis sit by the short-wave radio that brought news of thousands of prisoners around the world. The penny postcards they sent out (inset) were often the first word families had of their missing men.

For thousands of American and Canadian prisoners of war and their families, James MacMannis was a vital link in their communications across the barbed wire. Between 1941 and 1945, MacMannis, who had been an inventor, barnstormer and Coastguardsman, tuned his short-wave radio receiver, based in Florida, to monitor 33,000 messages from POWs held in Axis countries. The captors broadcast messages from the prisoners as a form of propaganda. MacMannis and his wife, Mary, transmitted the messages on postcards to the anxious families, who came to call the couple Mom and Dad.

Most of the messages simply assured relatives that prisoners were safe and well. Some, however, were poignant reminders that despite global upheaval, the blessed ordinariness of life persisted: "Sis," said one, "You can have my skates if you'll buy me a new pair when I get home."

nese guards generally left the prisoners to their own devices. POWs planted vegetable gardens, made paper from grass, water and ashes and—by tapping rubber trees, urinating on the liquid latex to make it coagulate, adding a little sand and waiting for the mixture to harden—fashioned quite durable soles for their shoes.

A personal passion—a hobby or other consuming interest, no matter how eccentric—carried many a man through captivity. David Westmacott, an airman who had been raised on the Dorset Downs of England, could be seen herding an invisible flock of sheep around his compound at Heydekrug in German-occupied Lithuania. An American lieutenant at a camp in Germany patiently counted all of the barbs on one section of the wire that imprisoned him and then worked out an estimate of the total number of barbs surrounding the entire compound. (His fellow prisoners did not think him wire-happy; in fact, they formed teams to check his count.)

Air Force Lieutenant Nicholas Katzenbach saw captivity as an opportunity for self-improvement. A navigator who two decades later would serve as U.S. Attorney General, Katzenbach set up an eight-hour-a-day reading schedule in the prison library at Stalag Luft 3 near Sagan, Germany. In two years he read more than 400 books supplied by the YMCA—history, politics, economics and literature. Princeton University allowed him to complete his undergraduate studies after the War merely by taking course examinations and writing a thesis.

The urge to while away the hours and days of imprisonment profitably also advanced the education and career of a young British artillery captain named James Clavell, who was not yet 20 when he entered the Changi camp in Singapore, which provided the setting for his novel *King Rat,* published in 1962. Even more significant, however, was Clavell's fascination with the people who were his captors. This interest culminated in 1975 with the publication of *Shōgun,* a best-selling novel about 17th Century Japan.

In rare cases, a prisoner's preoccupation became an obsession so intense as to threaten—if not actually breach—the border of sanity. Captain John Vietor, an American prisoner in the German camp at Barth, recalled in his memoir *Time Out* a Canadian pilot who became a fanatic reader of religious tracts. "Six months of rapt concentration loosened

his marbles," wrote Vietor, "and he came to believe that he was Christ. To keep peace, his roommates solemnly agreed with him." That the Canadian's derangement, despite appearances, was really a temporary mechanism for maintaining equilibrium eventually became evident. "The day after liberation," Vietor reported, "he returned completely to normal and couldn't even remember his delusion."

Perhaps the most effective means of keeping mentally fit was to find some way of carrying on the War despite captivity. In Germany, Allied POWs created camp-wide organizations to aid attempts to escape, reach home and resume a combat role. However, less than 2 per cent of all POWs actually attempted to escape during World War II, and the odds against success were illustrated by the most dedicated escapers of all—the men of the RAF. Of 15,000 British airmen in permanent camps in Germany, fewer than 30 ever succeeded in reaching home or neutral territory. But every escape attempt tied down enemy troops and absorbed the restless energy of the prisoners involved.

Some prisoners fought back—and tried to get home—not by escaping but by trying to outwit the enemy's doctors, feigning illness in order to win repatriation. Under the Geneva Convention, POWs could be sent home if they were certified as severely ill or disabled by a commission consisting of doctors from the captor nation and from the International Red Cross. The system operated on an exchange basis. The Germans, bringing home a similar number of their own disabled men from American or British captivity, repatriated several thousand Allied POWs for medical reasons. Most of these men were amputees and other legitimate patients, but a few were able-bodied, highly resourceful amateur actors. One was Flight Lieutenant John Leeming, who was repatriated from a camp in Italy; coached by a prisoner-doctor and abetted by a sympathetic Italian psychiatrist, he successfully feigned a persecution mania.

An elaborate masquerade pulled off by Richard Pape, a tenacious RAF sergeant, required props and special make-up. After several escape attempts—he once made it from Germany across most of Poland before being recaptured—Pape decided to change tactics and affect a serious kidney ailment. He ate yellow soap to make his skin look jaundiced and had a friend flick his ankles repeatedly with wet towels to cause them to swell. Then he constructed an artificial penis from rubber hose and filled it with the urine of a prisoner who suffered from nephritis, a kidney disease. When the doctors asked Pape for a urine sample, he surreptitiously removed the cork from the rubber hose and provided them with an appropriately unhealthy specimen.

In May 1944, the International Red Cross medical commission recommended repatriation for Pape, whose nephritic friend was also destined to be sent home. Traveling via neutral Sweden, Pape got his first taste of freedom three months later—precisely three years to the day after he had been shot down over Holland—when he stepped from a German boat onto Swedish soil. He was back in England two weeks later and soon returned to flying duties.

A repatriated prisoner like Pape was sometimes a valuable source of intelligence about his captors. Knowing this, American and British prisoners in camps in Germany fought their war by gathering information about the enemy. Where possible—for example, from one of many camps located near railroads—they maintained watches on train movements. They monitored nearby airfields where German experimental aircraft such as the first jet-powered fighter planes were being tested. In addition, by trading soap, cigarettes and other items from their Red Cross parcels with their camp guards, they gathered data on potential bomb targets, the scope of damage done by Allied bombers and details of antiaircraft defenses; they also picked up general information—prices, supplies, shortages—about the German economy. The prisoners then dispatched this news home via prisoners being repatriated for medical reasons or through coded messages in outgoing mail.

Prisoners who worked usually did so outside the camps. They were often in a position to fight back by committing acts of sabotage. At Osaka, Japan, Private Martin Boyle and his fellow U.S. Marines who had been captured on the island of Guam worked as stevedores on the waterfront. They took a perverse pride in their backbreaking jobs. These canny longshoremen were responsible for an impressive catalogue of subversion, related by Boyle in his book *Yanks Don't Cry*: "Crates and boxes of radio gear and electrical equipment slashed or smashed by cargo hooks and mishandling, rice bags ripped open when loaded onto boxcars, oil drums opened and drained in the harbor, boxcars derailed,

holding up a whole freight train, frail cans of medical alcohol ripped by sharp cargo hooks (and what couldn't be caught in small bottles and smuggled into camp for a quietly violent drink before a rice and soup supper, drained uselessly on a warehouse floor), bottles of acid dropped and broken, a few fires started, and one time a couple of guys jacked up a Japanese Army truck, took a wheel off and dropped it in the harbor."

In one sense the German captor's taunt ("For you the War is over!") was true: The War was over in terms of an individual's ability to contribute directly to victory, or to defeat. However, by trying to break his bonds, to gather intelligence, to harm the enemy in small ways through sabotage, or to simply stay alive and sane, the prisoner was prosecuting a highly significant war of his own. Recalling his experiences in Japanese-run camps in northern China, Major James Devereux, commander of the U.S. Marines captured on Wake Island, described one purpose of this private war:

"Hidden behind the routine, under the surface of life in prison camp, was fought a war of wills for moral supremacy—an endless struggle, as bitter as it was unspoken, between the captors and the captives. The stakes seemed to me simply this: The main objective of the whole Japanese prison program was to break our spirit, and on our side was a stubborn determination to keep our self-respect whatever else they took from us. It seems to me that struggle was almost as much a part of the War as the battle we fought on Wake Island."

In a larger sense, the stakes were life itself. The struggle was waged by numbers that shrank tragically as World War II dragged on. Of the 15 million POWs of all nationalities, at least six million did not survive. Some estimates of the prisoner death toll—from hunger, disease, neglect and outright murder—are as high as 10 million.

Among those who fought on behind barbed wire, there often emerged unexpected qualities of selflessness and quiet courage. Like many survivors, an Englishman named Geoffrey Adams, who was captured at Singapore, later tried to put into words the annealing nature of his prison experience. Nearly four years in Japanese captivity, wrote Adams, had "an effect on one's sense of values like the sea upon a piece of driftwood, stripping away all that is soft, leaving only the hard lines of the grain."

ORDEAL IN THE FAR EAST

Defeated British and Australian troops march under Japanese guard through a smoldering Singapore, past the bodies of slain comrades, to a detention camp.

A TESTAMENT OF HORROR FROM SECRET PAINTINGS

"No rest camp for British pig," said the Japanese officer to British artilleryman Leo Rawlings. "All men work, and work, and work." The words were a bitter greeting to Rawlings, captured in the surrender of Singapore in February 1942. Rawlings discovered the truth of the officer's statement when he was shipped, along with 61,000 Allied comrades, to the jungles along the Thailand-Burma border to build a railway in the valley of the Khwae Noi River.

Rawlings toiled in eight different rail camps, where he was required to work for up to 16 hours a day on a diet of watery rice gruel and vegetable stew, his body racked with dysentery and suppurating sores. He thought the job he had at first—hauling supplies from the river to the camps—was bad enough; then his captors sped up the work to meet a deadline imposed upon them, ironically, by the pressures of Allied victories.

Rawlings was assigned the backbreaking task of digging the roadbed. "We lived in a dream, by day and night," he wrote. "We awoke at dawn, ate our tin of slops in pouring rain and set out for yet another day of jungle hell." When he became too feeble to work, he was sent to a camp hospital—from which, often as not, the only exit was an unmarked jungle grave.

Rawlings lived to leave the hospital through the door, driven by a sense of mission as a witness. An illustrator in civilian life, he began to record, in paintings such as the ones on these and the following pages, the terrible details of his captivity. Mixing colors from the juice of jungle plants and fashioning brushes from tufts of his own hair, he depicted scenes of prison life: the fall of Singapore, the journey upcountry to the new railway line, the battle with death in the jungle hospital. With his companions keeping a lookout for the guard, he sketched by lamplight—putting anything on paper, even a diary, was punishable by death—and hid his paintings by day beneath his bunk. The result, which Rawlings later published in a book called *And the Dawn Came Up Like Thunder,* is a testament to the hardships inflicted on prisoners at the hands of the Japanese.

The Mae Klong bridge, nearly 800 feet long, is almost completed in this sketch by POW Leo Rawlings. It was a key link in the Japanese railway.

Footslogging where they hoped they would soon ride trains, Japanese infantrymen and mules move through the mountains on the Thailand-Burma border.

Prisoners jammed into open gondola cars for the trip from Singapore to Thailand swap their few valuables for food at a halt. A watch might bring a glass of water, said Rawlings, a spare shirt a few small bananas.

A work party trudges from camp to the railhead in Burma carrying supplies suspended from a pole. "Any lagging soon produced a dig from a bayonet point and a growl from the guards," Rawlings reported.

Four prisoners of war waist-deep in the Khwae Noi River heft a cross brace into position on a railway trestle. The logs, which were sawed into 10-foot lengths, measured approximately one foot in diameter.

Few men are on their feet in Rawlings' sketch of the hospital ward where he lay among desperately ill cholera patients—both prisoners and Asian workers.

Already sick, the artist has an abscessed tooth extracted by an Australian dentist.

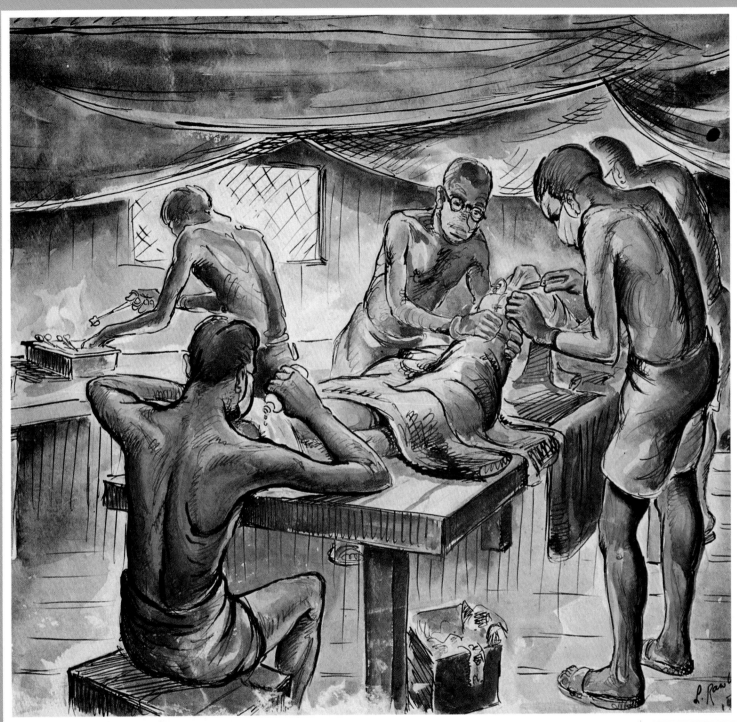

At a camp hospital, British doctors amputate a gangrenous leg in a makeshift operating room. "The stench of death was everywhere," said Rawlings.

The railroad completed and the jungle labor camps disbanded, work continues at other sites; above, prisoners fill in land for an airstrip near Singapore.

If the prisoners were lucky, these accommodations already existed when they arrived, having been erected by earlier groups. But most often they had to build their own, using handsaws and axes to cut the bamboo and the strips of bark that were used to lash the pieces together—the Japanese provided no nails. In some camps ingenious prisoners rigged showers from hollow bamboo pipes, but usually the prisoners bathed, when they could, in rivers or streams, using wood ash from the cooking fires to scrub themselves and jungle leaves to dry themselves. Their latrine was a large open pit aswarm with flies. Not far away was the kitchen, another open-sided hut in which they cooked their meager rations in an iron pot over a dugout fireplace.

Work on the railway proper began in earnest in the autumn of 1942. Each camp was responsible for construction in a section that extended for several miles in either direction along the right of way. The least onerous work was in the areas nearest the Ban Pong or Thanbyuzayat base camps. There, on relatively flat and open terrain, the prisoners' first task was to build an embankment 50 feet wide on which the rails would be placed. With spades, picks and locally made hoes, the work gangs dug up soil and carried it to the embankment in wicker baskets or in stretcher-like contraptions made of rice sacks slung between two poles.

On the Khwae Noi River, conditions were much harder. The prisoners who crossed the Mae Klong on bamboo rafts to start work in the Khwae Noi valley found themselves fighting the jungle. The route had to be cleared by sawing and chopping down hardwood trees of teak and mahogany and pulling out their stumps, and by digging up towering clumps of bamboo. The bamboo was so stubborn that 20 men might labor all day to uproot one clump. The jungle-cutting parties sometimes had the help of trained elephants and their *mahouts,* or drivers. At a command, an elephant would push against a huge tree stump until the roots were loose enough for the beast to pick up the stump and carry it off between tusks and trunk. These pachyderms were the only equipment available to augment human muscle.

Building techniques were not totally primitive, however. The Japanese engineers did use explosives—blasting whenever they needed to cut through a hill or to carve a shelf for the railway along a cliff. But the explosives had to be buried in holes a yard or more deep, which were drilled by hand. To do this, one prisoner held a crowbar while another hit it with a sledge hammer. Then the crowbar was rotated and hit again. Using this tedious process of tap and turn, a two-man team often took all day to complete one hole. And when the Japanese engineers set off the explosives, they seldom worried about whether the prisoners had been warned to stand clear; the men often had to run for their lives to avoid the blast and the resulting shower of rock fragments.

The Japanese organized the men into gangs, called *kumis,* of about 20 men each; two or more *kumis* made up a *han.* Nominally in charge of each unit—and held responsible for anything that went wrong—were *kumichos* and *hanchos,* usually officer-prisoners. During the first months of construction, the men worked nine days and had the 10th day off. A typical workday began about sunup and extended as late as dusk, depending upon the job and the temperament of the overseers. Generally, the Japanese engineers and guards were harsh; Korean guards, recruited from a region long dominated by Japan, were even worse. All the guards carried bamboo rods to enforce their demands.

At one point, trying a more positive approach, the engineers instituted a task quota system. A *kumi* was detailed to clear a predetermined area of jungle or move an assigned volume of earth in a day. The prisoners liked this system and began laboring with such zeal that they often completed their required task by midafternoon. But the Japanese, disturbed by the sight of prisoners sitting around with nothing more to do, began increasing the day's task. "Soon task work was dead," recalled Alfred Allbury, an artilleryman from the British 18th Division. "We returned again to the old system—we worked only when we were watched or walloped." That way, of course, not as much got done.

The work, for the most part, fell to enlisted men—at least for a while. The rank-conscious Japanese found it natural to abide by the Geneva Convention rule against forcing captured officers to perform manual labor. As a result, officers were generally cleaner and better clothed, and had a much more comfortable existence than the enlisted men.

Late in 1942, a glut of captured officers on the Thai end of the railway put an end to such peacetime notions of rank-and-polish. The extra officers had been in command of Indian troops, whom the Japanese had separated from their su-

A POINT OF HONOR

At Changi camp, a prisoner signs a pledge not to escape that he has no intention of keeping.

In August 1942, the Japanese commander at Singapore's Changi prison camp issued a decree calculated to humiliate its Allied inmates. All prisoners, he said, must sign a pledge that they would not attempt to escape. To underscore his edict, the commander ordered the execution of four hapless fugitives who had just been recaptured after three months in the jungle.

During their training, members of all the Allied armies had been told that a prisoner of war's first duty—a point of honor—was to try to escape whenever possible. In Southeast Asia, a murderous jungle fenced in the prison camps more effectively than any barbed wire. Nevertheless, the dream of breaking free—and getting home or fighting again—gave the men a lingering sense of hope and pride. The Changi camp prisoners thus refused to sign the pledge.

The Japanese commander was furious. He therefore devised a swift and brutal tactic to break their will. He herded the entire camp population of 17,300 prisoners into Selarang Barracks near Changi. The barracks were now accommodating 18 times the number of men they had been designed for, and many POWs had to sleep on the open parade ground or take turns in the available barracks bunk space. Latrines that were dug nearby brought on an epidemic of dysentery.

After three days, the senior Allied officer ordered everyone to sign the pledge. He asserted that honor had been satisfied because the Japanese had exacted the prisoners' word by blatant compulsion and the promise was therefore not binding.

Crammed into Changi's Selarang Barracks and forced to sleep and eat next to freshly dug latrines, prisoners of war from Allied armies wait out their ordeal.

officers in charge. Much of the brutality could be understood when the prisoners saw how Japanese soldiers treated one another. Japanese military discipline was based on corporal punishment. Officers beat noncommissioned officers who picked on privates who, in turn, used the despised Korean guards as their whipping boys. The prisoners were at the bottom of the pecking—or beating—order. For them, punishment was often a rifle butt in the ribs or being forced to hold a 30-pound rock overhead; if the prisoner faltered, he was beaten. What made it all the harder to understand was the apparent capriciousness of many Japanese on the railway. A guard might brutally assault a prisoner for a transgression—real or imagined—and then offer his victim a cigarette or some other simple kindness.

The unpredictability of the Japanese guards and junior officers mirrored the behavior of those at the top of the railway hierarchy. The commander in Thanbyuzayat was Lieut. Colonel Yoshitada Nagatomo, a dapper little man who loved to make long speeches to the prisoners and to preside over parades wearing full-dress uniform. On the one hand, Nagatomo demonstrated his hatred of Westerners by his attitude toward the prisoners under his command; for example, he made it a camp offense for starving men to buy food from the Burmese. Yet Nagatomo was also drawn to Western ways. He had picked up some French while stationed earlier in the War in the conquered French colony of Indochina, and he insisted on speaking it in his meetings with senior Allied prisoners, even though he had a Dutch interpreter who spoke fluent Japanese. Nagatomo drafted prisoners to build a soccer field (the matches ended after the prisoners defeated his team, 4 to 1) and summoned Allied officers to teach him to play bridge. These pro-Western leanings found little favor with Nagatomo's superiors, who later called him back to Japan and court-martialed him for—among other things—fraternizing with the enemy.

The senior Allied officer among the prisoners working from the Burma end of the railway early in 1943 was Brigadier Arthur L. Varley, an Australian cattle rancher. A hero of World War I and a brigade commander during the brief Malaya campaign, Varley was as stubbornly courageous as Nagatomo was cruel and vain. He confronted Nagatomo at every opportunity, citing from his British Army *Manual of Military Law* the countless Japanese violations of the Gene-

WOMEN AND CHILDREN IN THE EAST INDIES

Swept into captivity in the surge of Japanese conquest in early 1942 were some 80,000 women and children, families of colonial settlers in the Dutch East Indies—later Indonesia. Separated from their men, they lived in camps similar to those used for POWs. Often crowded into leaky bamboo huts, they subsisted on meager rations of fish and rice and coped with shortages of medical supplies. Some labored to harvest rubber and repair airfields.

Help came in 1945 when the British, representing the Allies, arrived to accept the Japanese surrender and evacuate Allied prisoners, including the civilians. Succor came too late, however, for at least 10,000 prisoners who had already died. Furthermore, the liberators could not reach the 30,000 internees held hostage by Indonesian nationalists who had revolted against resumption of Dutch rule after the Japanese departed. Many of these internees remained in captivity in the interior of Java and Sumatra until the late 1940s.

A girl pauses while cooking on a crude stove.

Isolated in cells at a prison camp on the island of Java, women suffering from dysentery are made to keep their distance from healthier inmates.

Internees use primitive bathing facilities at a camp housing 3,600 women and children. All bath water—most of it collected from rain—was cold.

va Convention and warning his adversary that he would be held accountable after the War. Varley kept a day-by-day account of his encounters with Nagatomo and of the abuses that made them so necessary.

Varley's protests seldom got anywhere, but the Australian soon learned that if a demand could be sufficiently dramatized he might win an occasional small concession. Once, for example, he prevailed upon Nagatomo to accompany him on an inspection tour of a jungle camp where a leg amputation was taking place under primitive conditions. Nagatomo watched for a moment, then turned away. A few days later two cases of medical supplies arrived at the camp.

There was no escape from the brutality and neglect of the Japanese except death. In the early days, Nagatomo had locked Varley in solitary confinement until he signed a pledge that no one would try to escape. Yet the pledge was a mere formality, like the bamboo fences surrounding most camps. A dozen or so men tried to get away but were quickly recaptured and summarily shot or bayoneted to death.

Mail from home was generally withheld by the Japanese. The prisoners' only real contact with the outside world was maintained through clandestine radio receivers constructed from spare parts that technicians had salvaged during the surrenders at Singapore and Java. Thomas Douglas, a British signal corps officer and former technician for the British Broadcasting Corporation, built eight sets while working on the railway. Batteries to power the radios were obtained surreptitiously. One prisoner who drove a truck for the Japanese at a base camp took his truck's battery to bed with him every night, ostensibly to keep it from getting wet but actually to provide power for his receiver.

The Japanese regarded possession of a radio as a major offense—two British officers who were found with a radio were beaten to death—and the prisoners went to great lengths to hide their sets. Radios were concealed in the bottoms of water canisters, under sleeping platforms and in similar hiding places. In one camp the only radio was kept in the wooden strongbox where a Japanese cook stored the food he pilfered from stocks intended for the prisoners. He did not know it was there, and neither did most of the prisoners. It was customary in each camp for only a few prisoners to be privy to the radio's whereabouts—and many did

not even know of its existence. Those who knew referred to the radio as the "canary" or "dickeybird" and to the batteries as "birdseed." The news, nightly bulletins from the BBC, was also code-named; it was the "doover" (Australian slang for "whatchamacallit"; much of the prisoner lingo was Australian), the "gen" (British slang for information) or the "good guts," and it was quickly passed around by word of mouth. When it included such events as Montgomery's advance in North Africa, said Rohan Rivett, an Australian war correspondent who worked on the railway, the news was "a great light to pierce our darkness."

The prisoners also found other ways to pierce the darkness. Music was one of them. At Thanbyuzayat, the base camp in Burma, the bugler was J. B. Cole III, a jazz trumpeter who gave invigorating twists to the traditional military calls. And impromptu songfests might break out anywhere. The Japanese took a particular delight in "She'll Be Comin' 'round the Mountain," sometimes joining in the chorus, though the prisoners substituted the words "They'll be dropping thousand-pounders when they come."

Sheathed in bamboo scaffolding and aswarm with POW laborers, the massive steel-and-concrete span of the main Khwae Noi River bridge takes shape. The structure, which crossed the Mae Klong River near its juncture with the Khwae Noi, took eight months to build, then needed constant repairs because of damage from Allied bombers.

A few prisoners had pets. Some Dutchmen kept a cat; a British captain shared his food with a dachshund. One group of British had a dog that, as Basil Peacock put it, "was quite imaginary." They went through the motions of feeding their phantom dog, made it do tricks and, to the puzzlement of more than one Japanese guard, called it to heel as they marched through the jungle.

Hobbies or other special interests provided a diversion for many prisoners. A British prisoner who had been a geologist went about collecting rock specimens. Ronald Searle, who later gained fame as a cartoonist in England, practiced his craft by doing portraits for 50 cents each.

Amateur theatricals offered another pastime—sometimes encouraged by Japanese officers. Stanley Pavillard wrote about a lieutenant named Hattori, a peacetime lawyer and teacher at the University of Tokyo, who spoke perfect English. "He was fond of quoting Gray's 'Elegy' and, more unaccountably, a number of old political speeches by Lloyd George," Pavillard recalled. With Hattori's backing, the camp staged a musical production, complete with a leggy chorus line. Costumes were put together from odd bits of cloth and bark; wigs were made from old rope, and makeup consisted of tapioca flour and juices and saps from jungle vegetation. Pavillard wrote: "This was a magnificent show, attended by a large number of Japanese, who kept nipping behind the scenes to make sure that our seductive chorus girls were in fact prisoners of war and male."

Thanks to unpredictable prodigality on the part of Japanese at another camp, a British lieutenant named Geoffrey Adams and three friends passed one very pleasant day. They were driven under guard to the Ban Pong base camp to help load heavy lengths of bamboo on a truck. After they had finished, the two Japanese guards took them to a café in the nearby village, gave them money and then disappeared into a local brothel. That was at 10 a.m.; Adams and his friends spent most of the day in the café feasting on noodles, pork and eggs, and enjoying coffee and liquor. A Buddhist monk treated them to bananas and biscuits.

In the café they also encountered Fuji Hayashi, a correspondent from a Japanese newspaper, who asked them in

excellent English about conditions on the railroad. Adams told him. "He took a lot of notes," Adams wrote later, "and I even gave him my name. When we had finished he remained silent and pensive for a long time. Then he said tersely that no one knew of our conditions, but he would not be able to report them in his paper; with that he left to catch a train back to Bangkok."

Adams' story appears in his memoir of life as a POW, which bears the ironic title *No Time for Geishas*. In fact, though men on the railway lacked access to women, they did not seem to miss sex; their apathy was probably caused by malnutrition. An enterprising sergeant from Texas invested in salacious postcards and tried to rent them out at a penny an hour, but he apparently found few customers.

Aside from food, which preoccupied their waking moments and often haunted their dreams, the men most craved tobacco. Hungry men would actually barter some of their meager rations for a cigarette. Tobacco sometimes could be obtained from the native traders, but the prisoners had to provide their own cigarette papers. The pages of many a book went up in smoke for this purpose. Much to the consternation of the chaplains among the prisoners, Bibles and prayer books were especially prized for wrapping tobacco because they were printed on fine rice paper.

The best time of a prisoner's life was the one day off in every 10. One of the most memorable of these days occurred in February 1943 when Australians at Konkuita, a camp far up the Khwae Noi valley, staged a jungle version of their nation's premier horse race, the Melbourne Cup. POW vendors sold peanuts, gingerroot flavored with palm sugar, and synthetic coffee concocted from burned rice. Colonel George Ramsay took the role of the Australian governor-general and even had a prisoner dolled up as the "governor's lady" on his arm. The jockeys wore scraps of native sarongs and colorful scarves that the men had purchased as presents before they were taken prisoner; they rode horses made of bamboo that resembled the hobby horses children fashion from broomsticks. Bookies took wagers, some of which amounted to a month's prison pay.

Such diversions made life on the railway bearable but, as one of the Melbourne Cup participants, Rohan Rivett, later wrote, they constituted "merely the odd pebble on the drea-ry expanse." Sick, hungry, exhausted, many of the prisoners had worked on the railway for nearly six months by the spring of 1943, and they could scarcely imagine things getting any worse. But a still greater ordeal lay ahead. This new agony came to be known as "speedo." Speedo was the way the Japanese pronounced "speed"; it was the one English word that every guard knew. On the Thailand-Burma railway the word had always meant "hurry up, *move it!*" Now it came to mean something more ominous.

By February of 1943 Guadalcanal had fallen to the Americans and the Japanese had been defeated in Papua New Guinea. Allied submarines were taking an increasing toll of the Japanese ships plying the roundabout route to Burma. Allied planes had begun to bomb the new rail line, which was in operation for only about 30 miles at each end and which, on the Thai side, ran just to the new wooden bridge on the Mae Klong. There were threats of British action to be launched from India, and the Japanese were sure that air raids on the railway would increase, slowing construction when the need for the track was becoming ever more urgent. The Japanese planners saw one hope: The monsoon season—bringing heavy, almost unceasing rain from May to October—would keep Allied planes on the ground. But the railroad would have to be completed and in operation before the rains ended.

In February the Japanese decided that the original November 1943 target for completion of the line was too late. It was now decreed that the railway would be finished by August. Speedo.

The new deadline meant that the 50,000 men already on the railroad would have to work even longer hours. Rest days were canceled. The working day was extended to 16 hours or more. Double shifts were started in some camps, and men labored through the night in the glare of bamboo fires and carbide lamps. Speedo also required a vast increase in the work force. During April and May, more than 10,000 additional British and Australian POWs were brought in by rail from Singapore. Many of them were assigned to the most difficult section of the route, at the head of the Khwae Noi valley near Three Pagodas Pass.

At the same time, the Japanese recruited or dragooned more than 250,000 civilian laborers from all over Southeast Asia to work on the railroad. Burmese were conscripted, as were Thais, Chinese, Malays and members of an Asian ethnic group called Tamils, who hailed originally from south India and Ceylon; many of these people had been brought in before the War to work on the rubber plantations of Malaya. The Japanese lured them to Burma by false promises of good pay and extra rations; the economy under Japanese occupation was depressed, and it probably did not take much to persuade these rubber workers to seize an opportunity. In Java, young men were tricked into attending free movies, then surrounded and hauled off to boats for the trip to Burma. Soon the Asians, including some women and children, found themselves working—and dying—alongside their former Dutch and British masters.

As planned, the beginning of speedo coincided with the season's first heavy tropical showers, harbingers of the coming of the monsoon and new misery for all of the railway's prisoners—the veterans, the newcomers from Singapore, and the civilians who were now arriving. On May 22 the monsoon began, and for 16 days in a row rain fell almost without letup. The Khwae Noi River became a torrent, disrupting the boat traffic upon which many camps depended for their regular rations and for the extras sold by the local traders. The camps turned into quagmires; the terrain along the railway became so slick with mud that prisoners used bamboo canes like ski poles to help them climb up and down the steeper slopes. One moment the workers would be scorched by temperatures as high as 120° F.; then the rains would come, turning bare backs and legs numb with the cold. Old uniforms were in shreds and nearly all the prisoners were reduced to wearing loincloths.

Three weeks after the coming of the monsoon, during a break in the weather, the War brought another kind of calamity. Half a dozen Allied Liberator bombers appeared over Thanbyuzayat. About 3,000 patients lay in the 14 bamboo huts that served as the base-camp hospital, but everyone who could crawl out of bed ran outside to get a look at the planes. Then the bombs fell. The targets were the railway sidings, Japanese barracks and supply sheds, but the hospital, unmarked by the sign of the Red Cross, was nestled between the sidings and the buildings. Nine prisoners were killed. Three days later, the bombers came again; 17 prisoners died and many more were injured, including Arthur Varley, who was knocked unconscious. Through an eloquent Dutch interpreter named Erik Leeuwenburg, Varley finally persuaded Colonel Nagatomo to evacuate the hospital so the prisoners would be spared further air raids and be available for work. But Nagatomo forced most of the sick to march 20 miles along the railway to a new camp; the journey claimed more lives than had the bombs.

The next blow to descend upon the prisoners during speedo was more insidious. Cholera was endemic in eastern Asia during the monsoon. The bacterium that causes it, *Vibrio cholerae,* is waterborne. It can be eliminated by careful hygiene—boiling all drinking water, for example, and sterilizing cooking and eating utensils. However, in the primitive conditions that prevailed along the Khwae Noi River during the summer of 1943, especially in the civilian camps, *V. cholerae* proliferated.

The epidemic first struck the camps near the Thailand-Burma border in May, and the news of it generated terror all along the Khwae Noi. The first symptoms of cholera—stomach cramps, vomiting, watery stools—are much like those of dysentery, which was common among the prisoners. But now, said John Coast, a British officer, "the slightest queasiness in the stomach sent men pale with fear." They had reason to dread the disease: In the advanced stages of cholera the abdominal muscles contract so violently that individual muscle fibers snap, causing pain almost beyond endurance. The body quickly becomes dehydrated and the soft tissues shrink. For the prisoners, death was a matter of only a few hours or days away, and it was almost welcome.

To fight the epidemic, Allied doctors segregated the cholera victims in isolation huts and tried to replace lost body fluids by pumping 10 or more pints of saline solution intravenously into each patient every day. Some were saved. Those who died had to be cremated to prevent the spread of the disease. Each camp now had its nightly procession of ragged men, themselves often near death, bearing the bodies of their comrades to the pyre of bamboo. In the heat of the fire, the sinews of the corpses would contract, causing the dead men to move as if alive. "While the flames crackled around them in the shimmering heat," wrote one witness, "they would turn, kick, bend and reach, then rise in a macabre dance—their eerie dance of farewell."

The Japanese defended themselves against disease as best

they could; they retreated behind gauze masks and bamboo fences erected to protect their living quarters from the unseen intruder. Better food and sanitation were their true shields, but some succumbed anyway. As work on the railway ground to a virtual halt, the Japanese came to realize that if the disease was not stopped, all hope of progress on the railroad would end. At last they flew in enough anti-cholera serum to inoculate the Japanese and most of the prisoners, and by August the serum and the Allied doctors' sanitary discipline had brought the epidemic under control.

Cholera took its greatest toll among the Asian civilian workers. Entire camps were wiped out. The civilians had no inoculations, no leaders or organization, no medical officers to enforce the sanitation that was the Allied prisoners' principal defense against the epidemic. The folk customs of the people created other problems. The Tamils, for instance, traditionally left their cholera victims in the jungle in a rough, two-foot-high shelter of rags, bark or leaves. If the victim got better, he crawled back to camp; otherwise he died and his body decomposed, contaminating the area around him. To protect themselves from the spread of infection, the Allied prisoners took on the burden of burying or burning the remains of the dead Tamils.

Aside from the Asian civilians, the men who suffered most in the cholera season of 1943 were the 10,000 POWs who had come from Singapore during April and May, when speedo began. They had arrived woefully unprepared for what they would find. They had heard nothing about the railway and believed still-current talk about "rest camps" in Thailand—rumors the Japanese helped spread. The prisoners had brought many of their sick comrades and considerable excess baggage, including several pianos. The pianos were discarded when the men detrained at Ban Pong.

Many of these newcomers had to march 180 miles from Ban Pong to jungle and mountain areas just south of the Thailand-Burma border where construction had not yet started. As they struggled up the Khwae Noi valley, the ill among them and more of their gear fell by the wayside. Once in place, they slept in old, leaky tents or in the open and were put to work on the railway before they could even build bamboo huts. Unaccustomed to jungle living and with little time to learn, they were highly susceptible to cholera and other diseases. Within a month, several of the newcomers' dozen or so camps had to be closed because they contained so many desperately ill men—up to 75 per cent in some cases. In all, 4,000 men—40 per cent of the new arrivals—failed to survive the building of the railway.

During the summer of 1943, the death toll in the camps all along the railway was increased by the official Japanese attitude toward the sick, an attitude summed up in an extraordinary order issued by Colonel Sijuo Nakamura when he took command of prisoners on the Thai side at the beginning of the summer. Nakamura's order cited the Japanese maxim that "health follows will" and asserted in stumbling English: "Those who fails to reach objective in charge by lack of health and or spirit, is considered in Japanese Army as most shameful deed."

Though the Japanese also applied this mind-over-matter philosophy to themselves, they translated it, for the prisoners, into a policy of punishment for illness. Those too sick to work were deprived of their pay, and their food rations were reduced. Under the speedo pressure to complete the railway, the Japanese fixed rigid daily quotas for the number of

After the last rail has been nailed down with a golden spike (above, in a commemorative replica), two Japanese officers in charge of building the Thailand-Burma railway report to the Army's chief of staff, Lieut. General K. Shimizu (center). Though the line was intended to carry 3,000 tons of supplies a day into Burma, severe maintenance problems caused by hasty construction often closed it down.

workers needed and routed out even seriously ill men to meet those quotas. In some camps, men were carried to work on stretchers.

The protection of the sick from the Japanese, as well as from the ravages of illness, was the job of the weary Allied medical officers. Each morning at roll call they had to provide the Japanese with their daily quota of workers and at the same time prevent the most seriously ill from being hauled off to the railway. (One problem was that some prisoners did malinger; in a few camps, ill prisoners sold their watery feces to other men who used them as proof of dysentery.)

To balance even minimal obedience to Japanese demands with the real medical situation required great tact in bargaining with the Japanese. One of the most effective practitioners of the art was Rowley Richards, an Australian physician who had learned to speak Japanese so he could argue more effectively on behalf of his patients. The daily confrontation between Richards and the Japanese noncommissioned officer at a camp in Burma was vividly recorded by an admiring witness, Roy Whitecross, in his book *Slaves of the Son of Heaven:*

"Often after much argument the Japanese NCO would announce, 'I will inspect the sick men.'

"So the sick were lined up and the 'auctions,' as Rowley grimly called them, commenced.

" 'This man has malaria now. He cannot work for six days.'

" 'One day,' the Japanese would reply.

" 'No, four days,' was Rowley's bid.

" 'Two days.'

" 'Well, three days.'

" 'Hai.' ('Okay.')

"To himself, Rowley would say, 'Sold,' and then move on to the next man."

The courage and concern of the doctors, many of whom were ill too, helped bolster the morale of prisoners who had almost given up hope. Doctors invented falsely optimistic news about the progress of the War, ordered sick men to recover, even threatened to court-martial them posthu-

mously if they died—anything to inspire the will to live.

That idea, the will to live—the Western equivalent of "health follows will"—appears again and again in the memoirs of those who survived speedo. Men often died, these accounts insist, simply because they gave up the struggle. "Once you bleeding well give up fighting, mate," said a British prisoner, "you've had it good and proper." Many men were sustained by their comrades, others by memories of home. Leo Rawlings, a British artilleryman, recalled a friend who survived cholera by propping a tiny photograph of his wife at the head of his bamboo bed and saying over and over again, "I *will* come home to you."

Royal Artillery Major Basil Peacock kept up his spirits by reading, having saved a few favorite books. He clung particularly to *Alice's Adventures in Wonderland* and "found there more sanity than was apparent in the whole of this crazy life of a prisoner in the East." Ray Parkin, an Australian sailor who drew sketches of life and death on the railway, wrote: "I am trying to find out how many vitamins there are in beauty. I am beginning to understand, as a pure-

ly factual statement, 'Man shall not live by bread alone.'"

Something of the same understanding came that summer to Ernest Gordon, a company commander in the Scottish 93rd Highlanders who had helped bridge the Mae Klong the previous winter. At Chungkai camp, Gordon lay in the Death House, as the hospital hut was called. He had diphtheria, dysentery and malaria, and his legs were partially paralyzed. The doctors had given up hope, but Gordon suddenly found himself stubbornly resisting the idea of dying. With the help of friends, he recovered and learned to walk again. He began to minister to the sick and dying. He helped massage paralyzed legs, taught Greek and ethics, and—though he had not previously been particularly religious—preached the New Testament from a bamboo altar in a jungle "church without walls." Gordon, who was ordained after the War, later served as Dean of the Chapel at Princeton University. "Suffering no longer locked us up in a prison house of self-pity," he wrote of those days at Chungkai, "but brought us into what Albert Schweitzer called the 'fellowship of those who bear the mark of pain.'"

By September of 1943, when news of Italy's surrender cheered those with access to a clandestine radio, scarcely a prisoner had avoided "the mark of pain." Speedo was at its peak. "By day and by night," wrote Russell Braddon, "parties of men, naked except for their G-strings and the canvas bandages round their ulcers, marched to the cuttings and the embankments and the bridgeworks of the railway. Their joints stood out grotesquely as they walked stiffly by, all grace and rhythm gone from bodies which, though still young, looked as old as Death itself."

By early October they had nearly finished the railway. Only a few miles of track remained to be laid. In the final days, Roy Whitecross recalls being in a group that worked 33 hours without a break. The rails and the crossties were loaded on small flatbed rail cars, or bogies, pushed by a makeshift engine—a diesel truck with interchangeable wheels that could travel on road or track. As the work train rolled to the end of the track, rails and ties were manhandled and set roughly in place at 30-foot intervals.

At 3 p.m. on October 17, 1943—just over a year after the beginning of construction—the last rails were spiked into place near Konkuita, on the Khwae Noi about 25 miles southeast of the Burma border. Fortunately for the Japanese the two ends met; several months earlier they had discovered and frantically rectified a surveying miscalculation that would have caused the Burmese and Thai sections to miss each other by about half a mile.

The Japanese celebrated. Up the new track from Ban Pong steamed a party of Japanese dignitaries traveling in a strange-looking train. Behind a hybrid truck-locomotive came three open rail cars roofed with palm leaves and bamboo; they looked so primitive that hooting prisoners called the train the Flying Kampong—a Malay word that refers to a group of huts. The occupants of the Flying Kampong debarked at the junction point near Konkuita to conduct an inaugural ceremony, and the healthiest prisoners were invited to participate for the benefit of photographers. A senior Japanese officer fitted a special copper rail to the junction point and affixed it with a golden spike, which soon disappeared—said to have been stolen by a prisoner.

The Flying Kampong was followed by a brothel train bringing Japanese women who dispensed their favors to the guards along the railway. At one camp, the prostitutes took pity on a group of British prisoners and distributed to them the money and cigarettes they had earned the night before.

The Japanese authorities were less magnanimous. They ordered the prisoners to hold memorial services for those who had died building the railway, and insisted on taking part. In the Burma camps a speech was read on behalf of Colonel Nagatomo, who wrote, "I have always done my utmost to discharge my duties conscientiously." Some prisoners got what they called, in a sarcastic reference to Hideki Tojo, Japan's Prime Minister, a "Tojo presento"—a pair of rubber boots, cheap cotton shorts or a can of fish.

The prisoners were not mollified. Thousands of their compatriots had died on the railroad, and the survivors knew that they faced further ordeals. Many of them remained in the jungle, cutting wood for the railroad's ancient steam locomotives and attempting to repair damage that rendered the tracks virtually useless for weeks at a time when the Allied bombers came in 1944. (By early 1945, it would take nearly a month for a supply train to traverse the route from Ban Pong to Thanbyuzayat.)

Thousands of the fittest prisoners were shipped off to Japan to labor in the mines and factories of the home islands. On his way through Singapore to board ship for Japan, Brigadier Varley managed to make contact with senior British officers at Changi camp, and he left his diaries with them. The documents were buried at Changi.

Varley was aboard one of two ancient freighters making up a convoy that left Singapore for Japan on September 6, 1944, carrying 2,218 survivors of the railway. The ships bore no special markings. Six days later the two ships were attacked by American submarines, and both went down. Japanese vessels recovered about 650 men, and U.S. submarines rescued 159, some of whom had been clinging to rafts and other debris for five days. These men became the first veterans of the railway to return to Allied hands, and their stories provided the shocking news of the conditions under which it had been constructed.

Among the nearly 1,500 prisoners lost in this tragedy at sea was Brigadier Arthur Varley. His diaries remained, however. Dug up after the Japanese capitulation in 1945, the documents helped to incriminate Varley's old adversary, Colonel Nagatomo—who, with 30 others, was hanged for his role in the railway of death.

Near death from exhaustion after three days adrift in the China Sea, an oil-soaked prisoner is hauled to safety—and freedom—aboard a friendly submarine. He had been bound for Japan, along with 2,218 other Allied POWs from Singapore, when his prison ship, the Rakuyo Maru, was sunk by a torpedo from the Sealion—the same boat that rescued him.

PRISONERS OF THE REICH

Americans in Germany, marking the end of a salesmanship course conducted by and for prisoners, celebrate formally with refreshments and entertainment.

CROWDED MEN AND EMPTY DAYS

Their German captors called them *Kriegsgefangenen*—a tongue twister that the prisoners shortened to "Kriegie." The jaunty nickname belied the grim facts of POW life faced daily by the more than seven million men—American, British and Commonwealth, French, Polish and Russian—held by the Germans between 1939 and 1945. Barracks, often jerry-built, were freezing cold in the winter and stifling hot in the summer; food was meager and unappetizing.

Most debilitating for the Kriegies, however, were the pervasive boredom and sense of futility. One American prisoner expressed these universally felt emotions in a poem: "The unused, empty days crawling slowly by/Each leave a question burning in the mind—/How long? A little while? For what?"

Kriegies coped with captivity as best they could—by reading and study, sports, theatricals and hobbies, and by keeping track of the world outside the barbed wire. Prisoners published camp newspapers filled with hometown items from letters and newly captured POWs and enlivened with hand-drawn comic strips and cartoons. They set up situation rooms equipped with maps and colored pins to trace the War on all fronts, using information they picked up on forbidden radios.

The Germans forebade much besides radios—proscribing tools such as knives or screwdrivers that could be used as weapons, maps of the areas around camps and any kind of photographic equipment. Sergeant Angelo Spinelli, a U.S. Army Signal Corps photographer, risked being shot for taking the picture at left and others on the following pages. He bartered American cigarettes from his Red Cross packages for a camera—smuggled into camp by another prisoner—and purchased film illicitly from a guard, using more Red Cross cigarettes.

Tidy administrators, the Germans generally segregated prisoners by nationality, rank and branch of service. Any contact between the segregated groups was prohibited, and the penalty for breaking this rule—even to help a fellow human being—could sometimes be death *(pages 66-67)*.

Bartering with a guard, an American confined near Fürstenberg trades a can of Red Cross-supplied margarine for a loaf of home-baked bread.

Cramped in triple-tiered bunks, French POWs try to make themselves comfortable in a camp near Limburg; such overcrowding of prisoners was typical.

APPEASING THE PANGS OF HUNGER

"Never during my captivity," said one American prisoner, "did I get enough to eat." Indeed, the German issue of rations, shown opposite, fell far short of the calories in the daily allowance for German POWs in the United States. The key to survival was the periodic Red Cross parcel, provided for most Allied POWs; the Russians, repudiated by Stalin, received no such supplement to camp fare.

The International Red Cross furnished meats and fish, powdered milk and coffee, cheese, margarine, dried fruits and sweets. Even so, many prisoners suffered weight losses as great as 80 pounds—although they were, in some camps, eating more and better food toward the end of the War than the battered civilian population in Germany.

A giant soup kettle dominates a camp kitchen at Fürstenberg. To augment German-issue kitchenware, prisoners made pots and pans out of tin cans that were recycled from Red Cross packages.

Three inmates do kitchen duty in a camp at Elsterhorst that housed 4,000 French officers. French prisoners received fewer Red Cross package deliveries than British or U.S. POWs and were not fed as well.

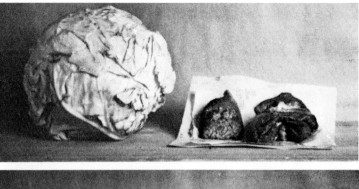

Photographs by prisoners document the meager German food allotment per week per man at Sagan. Mainstays of the diet were five pounds of bread and nine pounds of potatoes (top and above).

Other staples were two and a half pounds of cabbage and seven ounces of sausage (top). Grudging amenities (above) included bits of sugar, salt, barley, margarine, marmalade and ersatz coffee.

French soldiers grow vegetables at Stablack, east of Danzig. Lack of space limited gardening; prisoners usually had to barter with guards for fresh greens.

Furnished with books provided by the YMCA and other organizations, and by POW families, the library at Fürstenberg boasted thousands of volumes.

PASTIMES TO NOURISH THE MIND AND SPIRIT

Physical health was not the only matter of vital importance to prisoners; morale and general mental welfare were of equal concern. The Germans, anxious to head off trouble, usually supported religious and educational pursuits, as well as recreational activities ranging from drama to miniature golf. In some of the camps, prisoners gathered books sent by relief agencies and friends, and built libraries that were comprehensive enough to help them gain degrees after the War.

Athletics flourished among the better-nourished prisoners. Using gear supplied by the YMCA—basketball hoops, for example—POWs formed leagues in many sports. Sagan camp even boasted an improvised two-hole golf course.

Evenings were given over to theatricals. Although the offerings ranged from Thornton Wilder's *Our Town* to Shakespeare's *Macbeth,* the usual presentation was a variety show. The prisoners devised props, lighting and music that were sometimes of almost professional quality, with performances—sharpened by seemingly endless rehearsal time—to match.

A prisoner studies a scene (left), painted by a fellow POW, of Christ's descent from the cross. The picture decorated an Orthodox chapel (below) that Russian prisoners set up in their compound at Luckenwalde camp.

The smash hit of the 1943-1944 theatrical
season at Fürstenberg was the melodrama
Satan and the Soldier (right), a sprightly
morality play by an American POW.

Wearing improvised two-piece bathing
suits, wigs and top hats, a chorus line of hefty
prisoners enlivens a variety-show skit.

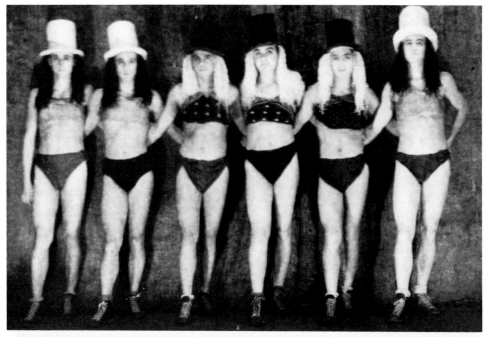

A scene featuring a night on the town, with fancy cars and pretty girls, dramatizes the dreams of peacetime life that were a recurring theme in camp shows.

A prisoner in a South Seas damsel's costume makes a convincing chorus girl. The POW photographer had to sneak this picture—and the others on these pages—after the guards and camp officers had left the auditorium.

A 1944 skit features a television set—a peek into the future of wide-screen video broadcasting. The set was the brainchild of a prisoner who, as a prewar employee of RCA, had worked on the development of television.

63

American prisoners of war at Sagan camp celebrate July 4, 1944, with a "bash" that featured gaming tables. The POWs could trade Red Cross cigarettes for gambling chips.

Middleweights slug it out at Stalag Luft 1, near Barth. The Germans encouraged such athletics—although the more poorly fed prisoners could not always participate.

A prisoner of war delivers a pitch in a 1944 softball game at Fürstenberg, in eastern Germany. Teams were organized into intracamp leagues, and the playing

level was occasionally superior—some men were former professionals. Handmade uniforms worn by a few players were usually saved for league title games.

Using a pole and a tin can, a French prisoner (background) at Stablack hands food through a double fence to a Russian. The delivery was strictly against the rules.

FORBIDDEN CONTACT— PUNISHABLE BY SHOOTING

Treated worse than any other group of POWs—and thus likelier to be punished for breaking the rules—Russian prisoners could expect to be shot almost automatically for communicating with men from other nations. Free-fire zones often separated national compounds; a man crossing the zone to talk or accept something handed through the wire was liable to draw fire. Yet such was the Russians' need—and such the pity their plight aroused—that other Allied POWs occasionally tried to help them despite the lethal risks.

A Russian POW at Fürstenberg lies dead—shot as he was trying to cross the strip of free-fire zone

between the stake at far right and the fence in order to pick up a cigarette that had been tossed through the wire by an American prisoner on the near side.

3

From the moment he was captured by the Germans on December 30, 1941, RAF squadron leader Thomas D. Calnan was a man obsessed. Though painfully wounded—his face had been seared black and his right foot broken when his Spitfire was shot down on a reconnaissance mission over the French coast—Calnan seethed with one desire: He wanted to escape.

For 40 months, all of Calnan's considerable energies were concentrated on that goal. He worked at becoming an expert picklock. He watched the sentries at his various prison camps in Germany, and timed their every move. Through letters written to his wife in a prearranged code he obtained a wardrobe of disguises, including a German officer's uniform made to order in London. It was copied from captured clothing and dispatched in one of the packages that families were allowed to send prisoners. Hoping that he could somehow steal a plane and return to England by the same means he had left it, Calnan committed to memory the cockpit layouts of a series of German aircraft, obtained from a fellow prisoner who had brought plans and specifications with him into captivity for just that purpose.

Time after time, Calnan tried to break out. Once, guard dogs sniffed out the tunnel he was digging just as it neared completion. On another occasion, when he was excavating beneath an asparagus patch that concealed his tunnel's entrance, the sand caved in and Calnan was almost buried alive. On three occasions he succeeded in actually getting away—by prying open the lavatory window on a train transferring him from one camp to another, by tunneling under the camp latrine, by strolling out the gate disguised as a Russian slave laborer. Each time, Calnan was recaptured and placed in a solitary-confinement cell as punishment. There he would begin plotting a new escape. He was still incarcerated and still plotting until the last days of the War.

Though Tommy Calnan never achieved the prisoner's coveted "home run," he rarely despaired. He wrote in a memoir ironically titled *Free as a Running Fox:* "For me, the fact of escaping, even if to nowhere, was a notable victory over my captors. Getting one up on them gave me enough personal satisfaction to make my imprisonment bearable for a long time to come." It was a thought that sustained more than one POW.

Successful escapes took luck. In his failure to make the

CHANCES OF ESCAPE

home run, Calnan belonged to the majority among the un-reckoned thousands of prisoners (out of the total estimated POW population of 15 million) who tried to break out of their confinement between 1939 and 1945. Escape figures covering all the belligerent forces are sketchy, but it is easy to see in the statistics for the armed forces of Calnan's own nation how steep were the overall odds against escape: Of approximately 169,000 British and Commonwealth fighting men imprisoned by the Germans in Europe, 6,039 officers and men got away and completed the journey to England. For Americans confined in Europe, of whom there were more than 91,000 from 1942 to 1945, only 737 officers and enlisted men managed to rejoin their own forces.

Success figures for Allied POWs in Asia are far lower, and most escapees came from camps in Hong Kong and Singapore. Such camps were close to the ocean, and beyond the surrounding areas were much more loosely controlled by the Japanese than was the case in Southeast Asia or the Philippine Islands—let alone Japan's home islands. When escapees were caught, the Japanese generally punished them with a swift and unpleasant death. The Japanese considered the role of POW a dishonorable one, and when they themselves were captured they tended to try suicidal mass breakouts *(page 15)* instead of individual escape efforts.

Axis soldiers captured in the Soviet Union found that the conditions of their imprisonment—starvation diet, harsh climate, the morale-crushing brutality of their captors and huge distances to be traveled—made escape almost impossible. The Germans generally treated captured Soviet troops the way their own men were treated; thus Russian POWs in Germany had much the same lack of incentive—or capacity—to escape.

For German and Italian POWs in Britain, the United States and Canada, life in the camps was not harsh, and its relative comforts may have dissuaded many a would-be escaper. But distance from home—an ocean away from North America, a turbulent channel to cross from England—and the difficulties of hiding and running in an alien land where there was no pro-German underground or resistance organization made for almost insuperable problems. No Axis POW ever escaped from Britain.

A few prisoners did make it all the way from North America, however. Perhaps the most notable German escape was brought off early in the War by Luftwaffe fighter pilot Franz von Werra. A swashbuckler who accorded himself the title of baron and kept a tame lion named Simba in his quarters as a pet, Werra was forced down over England in September of 1940. He made two unsuccessful escape attempts from POW camps in Britain before being shipped to Canada in early 1941.

To many Germans, the prospect of confinement in North America seemed to rule out escape forever: If it was hard to get out of Britain across the English Channel, how could anyone possibly make it home across the Atlantic? Werra, however, saw a chance in the fact that the United States, just across the border, was not yet involved in the War; he reasoned that it might be easier to find help and a place to hide there than it had been in England. On a midwinter rail trip from the port of Halifax to a prison camp north of Lake Ontario, Werra jumped off the train and made his way south to the Saint Lawrence River on the U.S. border. Reeling with exhaustion and numbed by the cold, he got partway across the frozen river before encountering a channel of open water. Ready to give up, Werra turned back to the Canadian side. There he stumbled on a boat hidden under the snow, pushed it across the ice to the channel, and drifted across to the United States.

More dead than alive, Werra was arrested by the local police for vagrancy and illegal entry, then handed over to the German Consulate in New York. As banner headlines blared the story of his escape—the Canadian government had made an offical request for his extradition—Werra slipped out of the country and made his way to South America. From there he sailed in neutral ships to Africa, then on to Spain and Italy before returning in triumph to Germany.

On the Allied side, the preeminence of the British as escapers was not really surprising, given their history, geography and motivation. The British treasured a rich tradition of escape. A brash 24-year-old war correspondent named Winston Churchill, taken captive in South Africa during the Boer War in 1899, had first come to widespread attention by escaping from a prison in Pretoria. World War I had produced so many British escapes that books published about them in England had aroused alarm: Letters appeared in *The Times* of London expressing fear that future attempts to escape in wartime would be doomed because so many secrets of success had been revealed.

During World War II, the map favored the British escape odds. The majority of British and Commonwealth prisoners (chiefly Canadians and Australians) were held in Germany or in German-occupied Europe; British escapers could blend more easily into the local population after breaking out than was possible in Asia, and once out they did not have far to go.

The prospects of a long war and a concept of rigorous military obligation also kept British incentive running high. Captured in substantial numbers as early as 1940, during the battle for France, they faced—as did French prisoners, still confined after their country fell to the Germans—a dismal future unless they got out. By contrast, Americans did not start populating German POW compounds in significant numbers until after the invasion of Europe in 1944, when the probability of Allied victory was already reducing the urge to take the risks involved in escape.

Throughout the War, a powerful stimulus for the British was their government's insistence that escape was a duty. Although all other western Allied troops, particularly officers, were given similar instructions, a special point was made of the obligation by MI-9, the branch of British intelligence responsible for monitoring and supporting escape efforts (pages 72-73).

Ironically, a contribution of sorts to the success of British escape efforts—and to those of other Allied prisoners as well—came from the Germans. Whatever they did to the Poles and Russians, the Germans were generally correct in their handling of British, American and Western European POWs. They permitted the International Red Cross to deliver food parcels, which supplemented the often spartan camp diet and made it possible for prisoners to maintain the physical strength necessary for trying to escape. Furthermore, the Germans typically limited punishment of recaptured prisoners to two or three weeks in solitary confinement (the Geneva Convention allowed up to 30 days). Part of this tolerance came from the German recognition that it was a prisoner's duty to make the attempt.

The German attitude was in sharp contrast to that of the Japanese, as demonstrated against three failed escapers from a camp in Java. They were stripped, lashed to the barbed-wire enclosure, and slowly bayoneted to death in front of their comrades, who were made to stand in ranks to witness the executions.

The Germans chose to emphasize prevention of escape, making their 90 permanent POW camps as secure as possible. Sometimes the camps (designated *Oflag* for officers, *Stalag* for enlisted men) were beetling old fortresses with thick stone walls and narrow, barred windows; some prisoners were housed in converted schools or factories, substantial buildings that could be made almost as escape-proof as a castle.

The camps specially built to house POWs were designed to foil escape efforts. They usually comprised rows of wooden barracks raised on pilings, which made the digging of tunnels difficult to conceal from the special anti-escape inspectors (or ferrets, as POWs called them). A double barrier of barbed wire up to 12 feet high surrounded the compounds. At regular intervals around the barrier were sentry towers with searchlights and machine guns. Guards patrolled the perimeter of the camp. They and the machine gunners had orders to shoot anyone who crossed a warning line within the compound, a wire usually set 30 feet inside the fence. The captors worked unceasingly to improve security. By 1942, German anti-escape measures included burying microphones in the soil in order to detect digging noises.

Patrols conducted surprise inspections of barracks. Some camp commandants even tried to plant English-speaking Germans as spies among the prisoners, a measure that often backfired when the stooge mysteriously disappeared. At one camp, the guards tried to prevent escapes by taking away the prisoners' boots and trousers every night.

German security officers quite accurately saw their battle with the best escapers as a contest of wits. They pored over old British escape books and set up "escape museums" displaying photographs of ingenious disguises and paraphernalia used in actual breakouts. They even brought in Franz von Werra to give them an insider's viewpoint.

In the early days of the War, attempts to pierce these German defenses were amateurish, "not a science but an emotional outburst," as one escaper put it. Individual prisoners would try to overpower a guard or slip through the barbed wire, often with tragic results. Soon, however, the prisoners began to organize, and escapes proceeded much like military operations.

At the heart of this system was a camp's escape committee, headed by a chief usually known as X. The committee coordinated all plans for escape, and a prisoner who wanted to flee had to register his idea just as in peacetime he might apply for a patent.

Once an idea was approved, the committee provided a wide range of logistical support. Prisoners with skills or aptitudes as artists and tailors were recruited to forge personal identification and travel papers for escapers, and to fashion clothing for disguises. Men with ability as traders and negotiators were supplied with coffee, chocolate and cigarettes from Red Cross packages. They bartered, bribed and blackmailed the guards to get German money for train tickets and good civilian clothes and to garner information about the best routes to freedom. Finally, the committee would organize ways of diverting the attention of the guards during an

attempted breakout—a boxing match, for example, a soccer game, or even a prayer meeting.

One of the more difficult tasks was forging papers. Early in the War, before the prisoners' organizations gained the scope and sophistication that made it possible to procure accurate models, such papers were almost flights of fancy. Planning one of his escapes, Thomas Calnan forged identity cards from pieces of cardboard cut from a stationery box. Despite the improvisation, the cards, he decided, "looked reassuringly official." The effect was complete after they had been lettered by a helper sufficiently skilled as a painter to imitate German typescript with a camel's-hair brush and black paint. On one occasion Calnan and a campmate, posing as foreign technicians, carried such a skillfully forged letter of sponsorship from the Krupp armaments complex that two police agents who saw it gave them a written introduction to a high Gestapo official and told them to call the man any time they needed help in their important work.

A severe problem was posed by the photographs required for some papers. These often had to be faked from newspaper clippings of pictures more or less resembling the escaper. At one camp in eastern Germany, however, the staff included an official photographer, a Polish citizen forced into the German Army after his country's defeat. His sympathies lay with the POWs, and the photographic supplies that he smuggled into camp for their benefit vastly improved the quality of their escape papers—as well as furnishing an accurate means for copying the maps that were so essential to a journey to freedom.

Unfortunately, the imperfections in these counterfeits usually were all too apparent. Careful official scrutiny of papers resulted, again and again, in discovery and arrest. The same problem afflicted the escape disguises the prisoners improvised. The least complicated camouflage was civilian clothes, which could be obtained by bartering with or bribing the guards or by converting old uniforms. Conversion entailed recutting the cloth along civilian lines; when the raw material was the heavy, blue serge clothing distributed to POWs, it also required long hours of scraping the dense nap off the cloth, which was then dyed with beet juice or with tints made from shoe polish and even from book covers soaked in water.

The rough-and-ready civilian disguise gained in reliabil-

In a tunnel-mouth demonstration staged for official records following an escape attempt, a German ferret—prisoner slang for the special guards who concentrated on anti-escape measures—holds the basic tools used by tunnelers: a piece of barracks floorboard for digging and a metal basin for transporting excavated earth.

ity partly because the dress of the people in Germany and the occupied countries became more and more nondescript and scruffy as the War, with its shortages and deprivations, continued. Another safety factor was the large number of foreign civilians imported from the occupied lands: By early 1945, to supply labor for their increasing war effort, the Germans had rounded up some seven million and put them to work in factories in the Reich.

When sufficiently authentic-looking, a military uniform carried more authority with status-minded Germans than did civilian clothes. But achieving authenticity could be difficult. Airey Neave, an RAF squadron leader who eventually succeeded in reaching England, encountered disguise problems of this sort on his first escape attempt from Colditz, the notorious maximum-security fortress in central Germany where the Nazis kept incorrigible escapers. Neave later described his maiden attempt, in August 1941, as "more of a theatrical performance than an escape." He was referring to his improvised costume—the all too obviously bogus uniform of a German corporal.

Neave had traded a month's supply of Red Cross chocolate for a khaki-colored Polish tunic; in the attempt to make it match German field gray, he applied green scenery paint intended for the camp theater. The result looked authentic enough in his dimly lighted prison quarters. But when Neave staged his "performance," he wrote later, the uniform "shone a bright emerald green under the arc lamps outside. I looked more like a demon in a pantomime than an escaping prisoner. The sentries laughed when they caught me and led me off to the cells." The next evening at roll call, even Neave's fellow prisoners broke into laughter when a German captain announced tongue-in-cheek: "Corporal Neave is posted to the Russian front."

Neave's next try was no laughing matter. His botched first escape had taught him that success depended upon "a minute mastery of detail." This time the plan involved a combination of disguises: a uniform to get out of the castle, and civilian clothes underneath for the run to freedom. Neave's German officer's uniform had a professional gloss. He had teamed up for his escape with a Dutch lieutenant, Toni Luteyn, and through him had obtained a Dutch officer's overcoat, which, though blue-green, easily passed for field gray at night. The shoulder braid for the uniforms the two

BREAKOUT GADGETS FROM MI-9

With a thoughtful eye on a gloomy possibility, American and British troops and airmen tried to prepare for German or Japanese capture by carrying into combat the maps, compasses, hacksaws, foreign currency and other items that an escapee might find useful. Thousands of men who were already imprisoned received similar paraphernalia, smuggled into camps in packages containing such legitimate materials as sports equipment.

Much of the escape gear came from a top-secret branch of British intelligence called MI-9, founded by Brigadier Norman Crockatt (opposite) to instigate prisoner breakouts. In many cases the items were the creations of an indefatigably inventive British intelligence officer named Christopher Clayton-Hutton.

Joining MI-9 in 1940, Clayton-Hutton developed a technique to reproduce maps of enemy territory on squares of white silk to be pocketed like handkerchiefs, and he designed a miniature compass that could be disguised as a service badge, button or collar stud—or hidden inside a fountain pen.

Clayton-Hutton's tour de force was an acetate plastic escape kit that fit in a jacket pocket. The kit contained a rubber flask and water-purification tablets, chocolate, a needle and thread, fishing line, a compass, and stimulant pills for staying awake.

Not all of Clayton-Hutton's inventions were successes. His escapee's flight boots, for example, could be modified to resemble regular shoes, but the boots became waterlogged on wet ground and were too flimsy for use in the air, where airmen's feet could freeze at high altitudes.

To smuggle in more prosaic equipment, MI-9 created ingenious packaging. Toothbrush handles contained hacksaws and screwdrivers. Money evaded detection by being slipped between the layers of metal in the walls of food cans.

On the receiving end, inmates quickly learned to spot special packages from fictitious donor organizations fabricated by MI-9 as cover. Among these "donors," a favorite was one called, with light-hearted irony, the Prisoners' Leisure Hours Fund.

Smuggled-in electronic components could be assembled into a radio.

Brigadier Norman Crockatt was the escape-minded chief of MI-9.

At MI-9, playing cards are pulled apart in preparation for the insertion of maps—printed on extremely thin paper—between the layers of pasteboard.

A FUGITIVES' AID NETWORK IN VATICAN CITY

British artillery Major Sam I. Derry needed help. He was holed up in a farmhouse 15 miles north of Rome, where he had hidden after he jumped off a train carrying prisoners of war from Italian camps to Germany following the surrender of Italy in the autumn of 1943. Some Allied POWs simply walked away from their camps when the Italian guards abandoned their posts; others, like Derry, were being shipped to Germany as the Nazis moved swiftly and ruthlessly to round up Allied prisoners.

Help came to Derry and thousands like him from a genial Irish priest named Hugh O'Flaherty, an official of the Holy Office at the Vatican in Rome. Derry, presuming that the neutral Vatican would have a British envoy, sent a message to the Holy See through a country priest, requesting aid from "anyone British." The Irish O'Flaherty was hardly pro-British, but he had been enraged by the Germans' harshness in occupying Italy, especially their massa-

cre of 320 civilians in the Grotto Via Ardeatina near Rome in retaliation for the killing of German soldiers by partisans.

O'Flaherty smuggled money to Derry, who sneaked into Rome hidden in a cartload of cabbages. He joined O'Flaherty to watch over a growing population of Allied fugitives until the Anglo-American forces could come to their rescue. Aided by a network of priests, nuns and Italian laymen, Derry and O'Flaherty made contact with Allied escapers, found them places to sleep, and financed them with funds largely supplied clandestinely by British intelligence. Special aid included smuggling a Scottish ex-prisoner in need of an appendectomy into and then out of a hospital aswarm with German wounded.

By the time Allied armies rolled into Rome in June 1944, the network had assisted nearly 4,000 Allied former POWs, including 1,695 British, 429 Russians, 185 Americans and 22 from other nations.

HUGH O'FLAHERTY: MASTER FUGITIVE-MANAGER

Major Sam Derry, British partner of Monsignor Hugh O'Flaherty in the Rome escape line, used this false Vatican ID card to pose as a fellow Irishman.

spare some of them so that the executions would not seem so much like cold-blooded murder, inviting reprisals. After the War, 14 Germans who participated in the shootings were tried by the Allies and hanged.

The murder of 50 escapers fulfilled Hitler's edict, but the actual choice of victims was apparently random. Among the dead was X, Roger Bushell. Among the 23 not killed was his old comrade, Wings Day, who was taken to Sachsenhausen, a huge concentration camp. Within 24 hours of his arrival, Day and four other RAF survivors of the massacre began another tunnel. He escaped with two companions, but was recaptured and spent another year in prison.

Less advantageous for mass escapes and far more risky than tunneling was climbing the fence. Indeed, the method was a form of suicide when carried out in daylight, though Allied escapers twice managed it during blinding snowstorms.

Success in the "over" method also was achieved by a prisoner at Colditz, a dashing young French cavalry lieutenant named Pierre Mairesse-Lebrun. Every afternoon, groups of men under close guard were taken for exercise to a barbed-wire enclosure in a park just outside the main walls of the castle. One afternoon in July of 1941 Mairesse-Lebrun was playing leapfrog in the park with several other prisoners. Suddenly one of the group knelt down near the wire and made a stirrup with his hands. Mairesse-Lebrun took a short run, put his foot in the stirrup and, with a boost from his accomplice, was catapulted up and over the nine-foot-high wire. He landed running, dodging the bullets of the sentries, then had to climb more wire in order to hoist himself over the park's 13-foot outer wall. Mairesse-Lebrun made it to neutral Switzerland, then across France to neutral Spain. Interned in a castle by the Spanish, he jumped from a window into the dry moat. The fall broke his spine.

Mairesse-Lebrun survived and, though permanently crippled, he eventually reached sanctuary in French Algeria. In his cell at Colditz, he had left his belongings neatly wrapped and addressed to his home in France. These were obligingly forwarded by the camp commandant.

The odds in favor of a successful attempt over the wire increased somewhat at night—even under the glare of camp floodlights. During the spring of 1942 at a camp for 3,000 officers and men near Warburg, about 20 miles northwest of Kassel, a British infantry major, Tom Stallard, pondered an impossible challenge: getting a number of men over the wire of an enclosure bounded by two fences about 10 feet apart. Then he came up with an idea. Like the best escape schemes, it was beautifully simple.

Stallard broke down the problem into its two essential parts: climbing the wire, and doing it without getting shot. The first part involved a major project in carpentry. Under the supervision of the escape committee, prisoners stole roof beams from a lumber pile inside the camp and constructed a two-part scaling ladder. One part, about 12 feet long, was an ordinary ladder; the other, about 10 feet long, was intended to serve as a bridge across the two barbed-wire fences. The whole contraption was built in sections so that it could be disassembled and installed on a wall to look like a series of harmless shelves. To test the plan, the men strung up heavy wires in a camp building reserved for music practice, erected the ladder and rehearsed their getaway.

On August 30, 1942, the date selected for the escape, the carpenters built three additional ladders and hid them in the attic of one of the huts. That night, a British Army electrician made his way to the fuse box—unaccountably left unguarded by the Germans—that controlled all the camp lights. Earlier, he had tested the second part of Stallard's scheme by tampering with the control box and putting the lights out for a few seconds. Now, once again, he plunged the camp into darkness. Out of the barracks rushed four escape teams, three of 10 men each, one of 11 men. They erected the ladders and, before a cascade of German bullets ended the maneuver, 29 men got up and over the wire. All but three were recaptured within a few days. These three, all Army officers, reached the Netherlands, where resistance workers helped them make the home run to England.

Breaking out through the wire was most enticing to those prisoners intent upon winning freedom singly or in very small groups. Though a courageous few actually attempted to cut through the wire, the exit of choice was the camp gate. One way out the gate was sanctioned by the Germans. Parties of working prisoners were periodically sent from the camps, either to nearby job sites or to temporary camps some distance away. The temporary camps were occupied by *Arbeitskommandos*—work groups of up to 100 prisoners who labored on farms or in mines and factories where security tended to be far less rigid than in the permanent prisoner pens. But the work, although providing opportunities for escape, was often so demanding that prisoners had little time or energy to prepare for a breakout; exiting via the *Arbeitskommando* route took patience.

The *Arbeitskommandos* were made up of privates and some noncommissioned officers who volunteered. (Under the Geneva Convention, privates were required to work; noncoms could perform only supervisory tasks.) Officers, exempted from work, often exchanged identities with members of the *Arbeitskommandos* in order to get through the gate. Several hundred such identity swaps occurred at Lamsdorf, a huge camp near Breslau that housed some 20,000 officers and men. Through this ruse, at least 11 men made home runs, more than from any other camp.

Getting through the gate could also be accomplished by stowing away. Scores of prisoners gained at least temporary freedom by hiding in vehicles that regularly passed in and out of camp—bundled up in laundry carts, clinging beneath trucks, even enduring in the stench of sewage carts.

Others capitalized on what one escaper called the German sentry's "astonishing tendency to take people at their face value." At Barth on the Baltic coast, after consultation with the camp's disguise experts, a member of the RAF walked out, masquerading as the civilian chimney sweep who sometimes visited the camp, in the sweep's traditional costume of top hat and tails and with soot covering his face.

At Spangenberg, a 12th Century castle just south of Kassel, three British officers succeeded in winning temporary freedom by posing as a German officer and two civilian members of an International Red Cross commission that periodically inspected the camp. At a prison hospital, Lieutenant W. B. Thomas, a New Zealander who had been wounded before being captured, planned to go through the gate by pretending to be dead. But when an orderly pulled the sheet over the prisoner's head and started to cart him away, Thomas could no longer handle the tension: He gave himself away by breaking into uncontrollable giggles.

To escape from camp was only the beginning. Most escapers were caught within the first few hours. Unless a man could fulfill Tommy Calnan's fantasy of stealing an airplane and flying to safety (no one did, though several got as far as the cockpit), he had to traverse hundreds of miles of hostile territory—both in Germany and, usually, in occupied Europe as well.

The hardest part, of course, was getting clear of Germany proper. Once he was outside the Reich, the escaper's hazards were still substantial, but the going was a great deal easier and there was even a possibility of getting help. On German soil, the opposite was the case. As soon as an escape was discovered, a description of the fugitive was flashed to security agents all over the Reich, including troops, police and the Gestapo, the Hitler Youth and groups of civilians known as the *Volkssturm*. Even if the escaper eluded those searching for him, he could easily run afoul of routine security checks; the Reich was a totalitarian state

In this sketch rendered by a prisoner of war in 1941, Colditz Castle's massive, ancient walls seem to close in on the small exercise yard. The thick walls at right and at bottom overlooked steep slopes. Prison cells flanked the narrow gateway at top, which led to an outer courtyard. The prison kitchens were at left, next to the storerooms.

where everyone was a suspect and everyone was—or seemed—suspicious.

The preferred mode of travel through this hostile world was the railroad, which ran almost everywhere and was, considering the wartime conditions, fairly efficient. Above all it was fast. The alternatives were buses—risky because the driver or passengers could get a good look at the escaper—and walking. Prisoners who tried to get out of Germany on foot found it much too slow; every extra hour spent in the Reich increased the chances of recapture.

Traveling by railroad, besides being fast, also helped alleviate logistical problems such as finding food—often available in stations—and a place to sleep. The worst part of rail travel, aside from repeated identity checks, was the waiting between trains. Trying to kill time unobtrusively, escapers

would walk the streets looking as purposeful as possible, or sit for hours in movie theaters.

The stress generated by this kind of pressure could be enormous. One morning in March 1943, after tunneling out of Oflag 21B near Schubin in German-ruled Poland—his sixth attempt—the inveterate escaper Tommy Calnan waited for a train at a station in Bromberg with Robert Kee, his fellow fugitive. To stay out of trouble, they locked themselves into adjacent pay toilets, munched their rations and wrote bored notes on toilet paper, passing them under the partition. But Kee was already feeling the pale anxiety that quickly replaces the first flush of freedom:

"I began to be frightened in a new way," he later wrote, "a way that was no longer amusing or exciting. Perhaps it was because we were now quite trapped if anything should go wrong, or merely because I was tired, but I now began to understand the full strength of our enemy. It was no longer just a matter of a few guards to be outwitted. A whole society was against us, and for practical purposes that meant all society, the whole world." His premonitions proved correct; after getting as far as Cologne, the pair was caught and sent back to prison.

Avoiding recapture was problematic at best. A million things could go wrong, and usually did. Sometimes trouble was brought on by carelessness, such as publicly smoking a British cigarette or eating Red Cross chocolate; one escaper was caught as he walked through a village in the middle of the night whistling an English tune. Other escapers were betrayed: A Polish sergeant in the RAF reached home in Poland only to be turned in by his brother-in-law. (The sergeant escaped again just long enough to kill his betrayer—which he did with no one the wiser—then he surrendered and was returned to camp.) When things went wrong, quick wit and steady nerves occasionally repaired the damage. Gordon Instone blundered into what appeared to be a waiting room in a rail station; when it turned out to be a German officers' dining room, he boldly walked over to the electric light switch, unscrewed the wall plate, fiddled with the switch, reassembled it all and then calmly departed. The German diners assumed he was a legitimate repairman.

Instone's charade succeeded because it exuded the aura of the workaday world. A different approach was taken by David James, a lieutenant in the Royal Navy, who deliberately chose a highly distinctive costume for his attempted getaway. During hours of enforced leisure in his prison camp near Bremen, James had spent a great deal of time thinking about the finer points of escape. "Escaping," he concluded, "was essentially a psychological problem, depending on the inobservance of mankind, coupled with a ready acceptance of the everyday at its face value."

James soon translated these abstractions into a plan. He already had decided upon the first stage: He would slip away through the window of a bathhouse outside the wire where the prisoners were taken once a week. He also knew that he wanted to travel to one of the German ports on the Baltic Sea, less than 100 miles to the north, where he hoped to stow away on a ship bound for neutral Sweden.

Pondering how to get to the Baltic undetected, James talked to Frank Jackson, a member of the camp escape committee. They decided that James's own Royal Navy uniform would stand him in sufficiently good stead once he arrived at the Baltic ports, where seamen were a familiar sight. But how could he explain his uniform en route to the Baltic? The answer: James would travel as the fictitious Lieutenant Ivan Bagerov of the Royal Bulgarian Navy. Bulgaria, a member of the Axis, was a monarchy, which would account for the crown on the buttons of James's British uniform. The only necessary alteration was to sew onto the left shoulder initials denoting the Royal Bulgarian Navy, which was so small—"about three ships," James estimated—that the odds were strongly against encountering a German official who knew what the real uniform looked like. Aided by the camp forgers, James put together an identity card complete with a photograph made from a newspaper clipping of a German Navy hero who vaguely resembled him.

In December 1943, James slipped away from the bathhouse and traveled by train to Lübeck, about 90 miles from Bremen. He performed his role brilliantly, passing all identity checks until a German sentry, seeing him prowling around the docks at Lübeck, brought him in for questioning. Back at camp, James ripped off the gold initials.

Two months later he tried again, still wearing a naval uniform, but this time assuming the identity of a Swedish merchant-marine officer. After reaching Lübeck, he bribed a Finnish sailor to stow him away on a freighter bound for Stockholm. There he contacted British consular officials,

who hid him in the bomb bay of a Mosquito aircraft, a fast, versatile fighter-bomber often used for courier duty of this sort. Disguised with civilian markings, the plane could travel between England and Stockholm without embarrassing the neutral Swedes. In a few hours, David James was home.

As James knew, reaching Sweden—or Switzerland—meant sanctuary. Under international law, neutral governments could—and sometimes did—intern or detain any citizen of a belligerent country, including escapers. But conditions were generally far less harsh than at a prisoner-of-war camp; getting away was easier and much less dangerous, and friendly diplomats from the home country usually stood ready to help.

Still, reaching sanctuary of any kind unaided—as James found out—was a chancy business. The odds improved if a man could make contact with one of a number of organizations called escape lines that were set up to speed safe journeys through occupied countries in both Eastern and Western Europe. Citizens who joined these organizations risked torture and death—no Geneva Convention protected them or their families from reprisal by the Gestapo if they were caught helping or harboring escapers.

Despite the danger, a number of escape lines were organized by resistance movements in Western Europe with the aid of MI-9. These lines funneled escapers to freedom, either to pickups by British ships or submarines along the French coast, or through the Pyrennees into neutral Spain and then to British Gibraltar.

One of the British officials responsible for these lines after June 1942 was Airey Neave, the British Army lieutenant who had escaped from Colditz wearing an ersatz German uniform. Like many others who had made it to Switzerland, Neave had been escorted through southern France and into Spain by members of an escape line headed by a former Belgian medical officer named Albert-Marie Guerisse, who took the *nom de guerre* Patrick O'Leary. The O'Leary line survived the betrayal and execution of more than 50 of its members to carry on its work until 1943, when a second betrayal put O'Leary behind the wire at Dachau, where he lived out the remainder of the War.

The eastern escape route, through Poland and into the Soviet Union, was the most perilous way out of Germany. Most Poles were willing to shelter fugitives, and members of the underground established escape lines that enabled prisoners to cross into the Soviet Union. There, however, the escapers were subject to the unpredictability of Soviet political attitudes.

Early in the War, many escapers simply disappeared into the east and were never heard of again. James Allan, a British Army corporal captured in France, had assaulted his guard to escape from a German camp near Torun in western Poland. He crossed into Russian-occupied eastern Poland in the autumn of 1940 before the Soviet Union entered the war against Germany. Allan expected the neutral Soviets to treat him with fairness and respect. Instead, they arrested him as a British spy, tortured him and held him in various jails, including Moscow's notorious Lubyanka Prison, for nearly a year before they released him and allowed him to be repatriated. Ironically, Allan's best friend in prison was a young German who had been captured by the Russians while on an actual spying mission.

The Russians were much friendlier toward RAF Warrant Officer Cyril Rofe and Army Corporal Karl Hillebrand, who had been held prisoner at Lamsdorf. Exchanging their identities with privates to join the *Arbeitskommandos,* Rofe and Hillebrand escaped in August 1944 from a project outside Schonberg where they were building bungalows. Wearing civilian clothes, they took the train eastward. Sheltering first with Polish partisans, then with Soviet partisans and finally

A Dutch officer displays an eerily lifelike plaster bust that was used at Colditz Castle to fool German officials at head-count formations. Following a breakout, prisoners would hold up the costumed bust (above) to provide a stand-in for the missing escaper.

encountering regular Red Army troops operating behind German lines, they moved gradually and safely eastward to sanctuary behind Soviet lines; from there they traveled to Moscow and were eventually repatriated to England.

Colditz. The name—made famous since World War II in books and a motion picture, *The Colditz Story*—conveys the grim nature of its purpose: to confine the most incorrigible escapers and make sure they did not get out again. It was the toughest POW camp in Germany.

The prison was built into a castle overlooking the central German village of Colditz and resting on stone foundations certainly dating from the year 1014—possibly before. Over the centuries new fortifications had been built upon earlier ruins. In the 18th Century the castle was the palace of Augustus the Strong, Elector of Saxony and King of Poland. More recently it had housed a lunatic asylum, then a concentration camp for Hitler's political opponents.

The commandant at Colditz considered the camp escape-proof. The outside walls were of stone and mortar seven feet thick. On three sides these walls stood upon a sheer precipice that dropped several hundred feet to the Mulde River. On the fourth side the main gate opened inward to a bridge over a dry moat. From there the way led through three successive inner gates of oak and iron, which finally gave access to the courtyard around which the prisoners were housed. To all this, the Germans added a few touches. They staffed Colditz with a garrison of guards and officers that always outnumbered the prisoners. They surrounded the whole structure with barbed wire and then slung catwalks, fortified with machine-gun posts, on the wall. To make certain their prisoners were always accounted for, the Germans increased the number of daily *Appells*—head-count formations—from two to four.

In theory, Colditz made sense; in practice, it was an invitation to trouble: In it were concentrated the Allies' most resourceful POW troublemakers. By 1942, Colditz housed some 80 British officers, 200 French, 60 Dutch and an assortment of Belgians, Yugoslavs and others.

Colditz was, in the wry words of a British prisoner, a "hive of industry," and that industry was escape. Each nationality had its own escape committee along with forgers, tailors and other workers. A Polish lieutenant named Nie-denthal even improvised a crude but effective typewriter on which to forge travel documents. A Dutch amateur sculptor carved from ceiling plaster two life-sized busts named Max and Moritz; these busts, draped with long officers' overcoats, were carried to *Appell* when two Dutchmen had escaped, fooling the Germans into thinking everyone was present and giving the escapers precious getaway time before the alert was sounded. The British stole colored lights from an attic full of Christmas decorations, then tapped the castle electricity to create an elaborate warning system to indicate the whereabouts of German guards.

So industrious were the denizens of Colditz that in October 1942, when Hitler ordered the handcuffing of POWs in reprisal after some dead German prisoners were found with their hands bound behind their backs following the British raid on Dieppe, the castle was exempted. German officials feared that the prisoners would merely add the handcuffs to their store of escape tools.

Among the most troublesome notables gathered at Colditz was RAF Wing Commander Douglas Bader, the legendary fighter ace who had lost both legs during a plane crash in the early 1930s. Bader was taken prisoner in 1941 after his Spitfire collided with a German fighter over France. A few days later he knotted together 15 sheets and lowered himself from the window of a military hospital in Saint Omer. After his recapture, Bader tried unsuccessfully to break out of several camps in Germany. Finally, he resigned himself to the fact that his legs, artificial from the knees down, would not carry him fast enough to get away.

Bader poured his frustrations into the practice known as "goon-baiting," behavior aimed at provoking or demoralizing the Germans. (In the British POW lexicon, any German was a "goon." The word originally derived from a large, stupid character in the Popeye comic strip, but prisoners liked to tell their German captors that it was an acronym for "German officer or noncommissioned officer.") At Colditz, Bader conducted his own propaganda leaflet raids, scribbling uncomplimentary messages in German on sheets of toilet paper and tossing them from the castle windows when the winds were blowing toward the village.

The camp officials were, in fact, by turns infuriated, awed and bemused by the enterprise of the prisoners in their castle. Captain Reinhold Eggers, a former schoolteacher who was security chief at Colditz for much of the War, later wrote (with a touch of pride) that during his tenure an escape attempt had occurred at least every 10 days. Eggers admitted that he did not know the details of some escapes until the escapers wrote about their exploits after the War.

Along with Airey Neave, one of the celebrated escapers at Colditz was British Army Captain Patrick Reid. Reid, who could "think of no sport that is the peer of escape," served as X, chief British escape officer, for nearly two years at Colditz. One of his first accomplishments was to organize a 24-hour "goon-watch" aimed at spotting the least weakness in the enemy's armor. "Every sentry's beat, every arc light's timetable, the entire routine of the garrison," noted another author's account, "were studied as intensely as any young lover ever watched the movements of the beloved."

A powerfully built man with a deceptively quiet voice, Reid imposed discipline on his group of British eccentrics with a forceful presence and a nice sense of humor. Once, he "borrowed" the camp dentist's drill and dulled a number of bits in a futile effort to grind a master door key: "Ever afterwards," he wrote after the War, "when I heard the agonizing shrieks of sufferers in the dentist's chair I felt a twinge of remorse that I should have been the cause of so much fruitless pain!"

Reid was an engineer in civilian life, and his eye for construction was quick to detect potential exits from the castle. After presiding over a number of successful escapes by others, Reid managed his own in October 1942. With three companions, he executed a complex plan that involved cutting window bars, climbing down into the dry moat and squeezing through an air shaft in the cellar of a German administrative building. The plan worked, and all four made it. Safe inside Switzerland within a week, Reid became an assistant to H. A. Cartwright, British Military Attaché in Berne, who happened to be a noted World War I escaper.

The Germans at Colditz considered a young British infantry lieutenant, Michael Sinclair, the greatest escaper of them all; they called him *Rote Fuchs,* the Red Fox, for the color of his hair and the range of his cunning. Before he came to Colditz early in 1942, Sinclair already had been outside the wire on two occasions. From Colditz, by German count, he made seven attempts. Once, in a carefully planned and executed charade that went awry at the last moment, Sinclair

posed as the German garrison's sergeant major, even imitating the man's way of walking and talking. The German sentry noticed one misstep, however, challenged Sinclair and, in the ensuing mix-up, shot him at point-blank range. The bullet went cleanly through Sinclair's chest, missing his heart by two inches. Less than five months later the Red Fox was at large once more, just short of the Dutch border, where a policeman recognized him from the photographs of escapers circulated daily throughout Germany.

Back inside the castle again, Sinclair brooded for eight months. Then, on September 25, 1944, he made his move. Unlike his previous attempts, this one he made alone, telling no one in order to prevent others from being implicated. That afternoon he was exercising with other British prisoners in the same park outside the castle where Pierre Mairesse-Lebrun had vaulted the wire three years earlier. He shook hands with a friend. "Good-by," he said, "It's going to be now or never." He dashed for the wire, scaled it successfully and was running for the outer wall when the cries of "Halt!"—and then the shots—rang out. It was Michael Sinclair's final break for freedom—in the words of a Swiss Red Cross representative, "an act of despair." Never again would the Red Fox be caged in the forbidding gray castle at Colditz.

By the time Sinclair made his fatal move in the autumn of 1944, the success of Allied armies in France was beginning to dampen the eagerness of most Allied prisoners to break out. But at Colditz Castle, even as the Allied armies converged on Germany in early 1945, the flame still burned. A team of prisoners headed by Tony Rolt, an imaginative British infantry lieutenant who had been a noted amateur race-car driver before the War, had concealed a huge workshop behind a false wall in the attic over the castle's chapel. There the men constructed from bed slats, floor boards and mattress covers a contraption that must have soared at one time or another in every escaper's fantasies—a glider. The craft had a 33-foot wingspan and was designed to carry two men. It was scheduled to be launched in the spring of 1945 from the roof of the castle, using a catapult powered by a mechanism that involved dropping a bathtub full of concrete 60 feet. On April 15, 1945, shortly before this incredible escape machine had a chance to get off the ground, Colditz was liberated by the Americans.

BEATING THE SYSTEM

Sharing two sets of civilian coats, shirts and ties, French officers planning an escape prepare to have fake identity-card photographs taken by a fellow prisoner.

In an extraordinary photograph taken by a prisoner, a comrade squats (left center) to confuse the guards' head count and conceal evidence of an escape.

KEEPING TABS ON THE ENEMY

Both prisoners and ferrets observed each other relentlessly—and both sides kept careful records of the surveillance. Ferrets especially valued photographic proof of their investigative prowess, and they used the pictures to train new ferrets in such skills as spotting sand that had been excavated from tunnels.

Meanwhile, prisoners kept minutely detailed records of their captors' movements. So thorough was the monitoring at Stalag Luft 3 that chief ferret Glimnitz jokingly reminded POW record-keepers of guards' arrivals and departures that he claimed they had overlooked. The value of the prisoners' logs was indisputable: An estimated 18,000 bags of earth removed from one tunnel were dispersed without detection because each bag was dumped in the few moments when records showed that no guard would be watching.

In an aboveground reconstruction, a ferret shows how a homemade tunnel trolley could haul sand.

Carrying bags of sand outside his trousers rather than inside them for a photographed demonstration, a German documents the prisoners' way of disposing of excavated earth.

A smiling ferret displays the efficient bellows-type air pump that ventilated the tunnel used in the most successful escape from Sagan. The pump made little noise and was capable of dispersing odors from the tunnel.

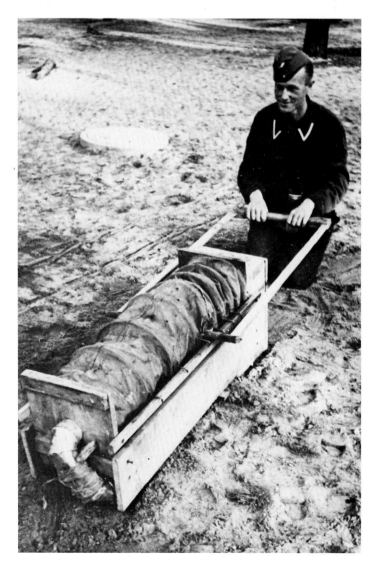

Glemnitz	11.00			910	945	1500	1925	
Blue Boy	11.50			850	1200	1805		
Phil	30.40			870	1225	1540		
Oscar	83.30			820	1230	1350	1710	1800	1900
Shorty				900	1200	1535		
Pop				815	1350	1900		
Frehwer				950	1130	1645	1715	
Grote				950	1130	1645	1715	
Hornhal				940	1435	1520	1715	1720	1800
1G	845	1035	1G				1520	1245
1G	900	925	1G				1620	1235
1G	925	1020	Kitch G				1625	1800
1G	930	955	1G				1630	1640
Marl G	930	1020	1G - blue coveralls				1645	1720
6 app Gs	945	1020	6 app Gs				1650	1715
2 Gs	950	1205	1G - coal wag				1650	1725
1G	1000	1015	1G - " "				1715	1730
1G - wag	1020	1025	1G - " "				1745	1755
1G	1025	1215	1G - " "				1745	1755
1G	1030	1045	2 Gs - " " (1 out 1910)				1810	1825
2 Gs	1030	1115	1G - parcel "				1815	1820
1G	1055	1100						
4 Gs	1107	1125						
1G	1110	1125						
1G	1120	1200						
2 G	1455	1522						
1G - wag	1510	1530						
Fri May 24								
Blue Boy	24.40			835	955	1105	1205	1520	1820
Phil	7.45			905	1415	1855	1955	
	45.50			855	1205	1500	1900	
	75.15			830	1205	1350	1715	
Frehwer				950	1045	1650	1930	
Grote				950	1120	1650	1730	
Hornhal				940	1210	1610	1740	
1G	855	1100	1G - coal wag				1100	1125
1G - wag	915	940	1G				1100	1110
1G - "	916	955	2 Gs				1120	1610
1G - "	916	935	5 Gs				1130	1135
1G	940	1025	1G, 1 driver - wag				1403	1451
Marl G	942	1038	1G				1525	1550
1G - wag	945	1010	2 Gs				1531	1745 1730
1G - "	945	1020	1G				1630	1455
6 app Gs	947	1015	7 app Gs				1645	1715
2 Gs	950	955	1G - wag				1730	1745
1G - wag	955	1005	1 driver, 1G - truck				1935	2010
1G - "	1000	1010						
1G - "	1015	1035						
1G	1005	1025	North compound British break big					
1G - wag	1005	1025	tunnel. Number of escapees unknown.					
1G officer	1005	1202	Rumored 80.					
2 Gs	1005	1202						
1G	1020	1030						
1G	1022	1045						
1G - wag	1024	1045						
1G - "	1025	1045						
1G	1027	1246						
1G - wag	1028	1100						
1G	1045	1307						
1G - wag	1050	1115						

This Ferret-Watchers' log, kept by POWs in the South Compound of Stalag Luft 3 at Sagan, details the minute-by-minute presence of German personnel. The top section for each day lists nine ferrets by nickname; the next section records the guards' movements. The log, dated March 23 and 24, notes a breakout from the British compound (lower right) with the comment: "Number of escapees unknown. Rumored 80."

A TENUOUS LINK
TO THE OUTSIDE WORLD

Just as thoughts of escape gave prisoners a sense of contact with home, listening to radio broadcasts on illicit receivers brought the world at large inside the wire. Other news sources were meager: Nazi loudspeaker broadcasts yielded little but propaganda, and letters from home were censored and were usually weeks late.

To provide prisoners with news, Allied intelligence authorities hid tiny radio parts in parcels sent from home. At the camps, skilled technicians assembled them, supplementing the imported essentials with parts made from metal and wood scrap.

One officer smuggled his radio into camp by leaving it in its carrying case behind a radiator while he was being searched.

Most camps had one or more clandestine radios, usually simple receivers. Prisoners tuned in the news from the BBC, which also broadcast an occasional personal message to prisoners—for instance, notification of a death in a family.

Because radios were so precious, they were carefully hidden from the guards—in musical instruments, in lamp bases and light switches, under floorboards—and in one case, inside a medicine ball.

Ingeniously tucked away in an accordion, a secret packet contains the components needed to assemble a radio receiver.

American prisoners of war in Stalag Luft 3 concentrate as they listen on their clandestine radio receiver to a news bulletin broadcast from Great Britain.

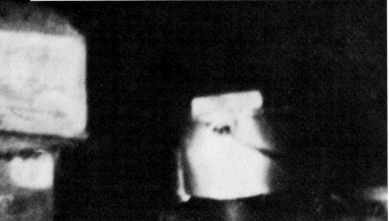

Taking advantage of an ideal match of shapes, prisoners hide an earphone inside a round light switch. Concealing components separately ensured that an entire radio would not be lost during a successful search.

A ladder leads to the tunnel called Harry. Of the 76 POWs who used it in the Great Escape, 73 were recaptured and 50 of them executed

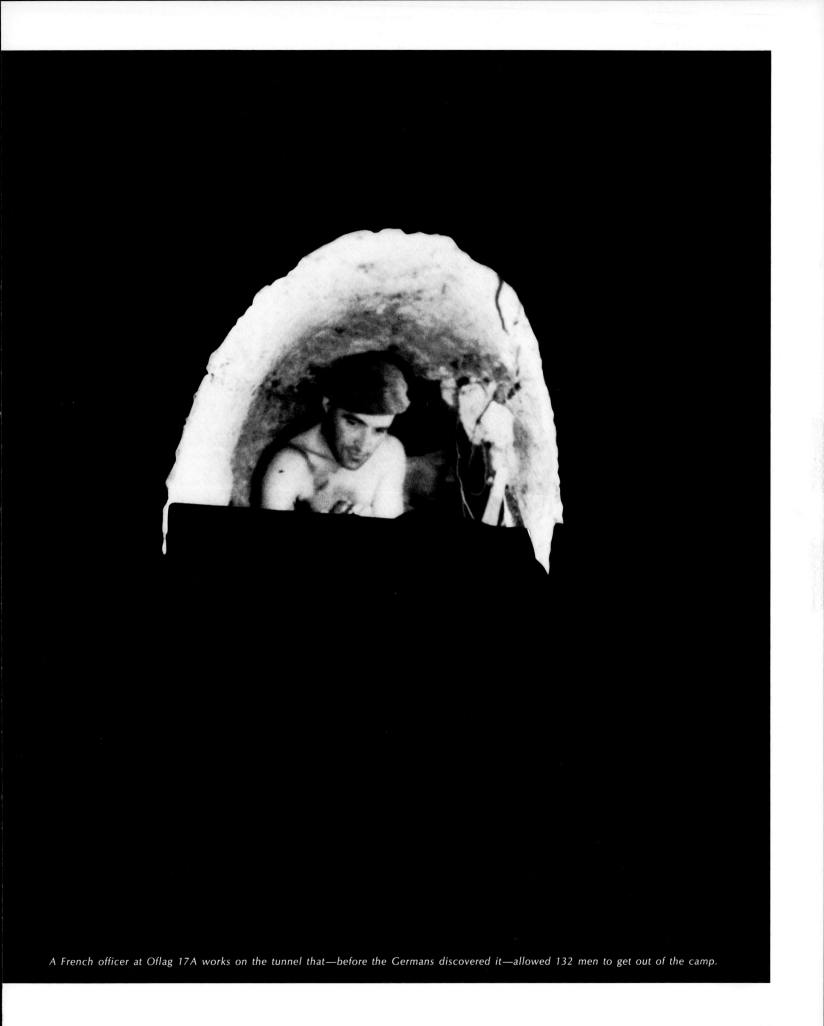

A French officer at Oflag 17A works on the tunnel that—before the Germans discovered it—allowed 132 men to get out of the camp.

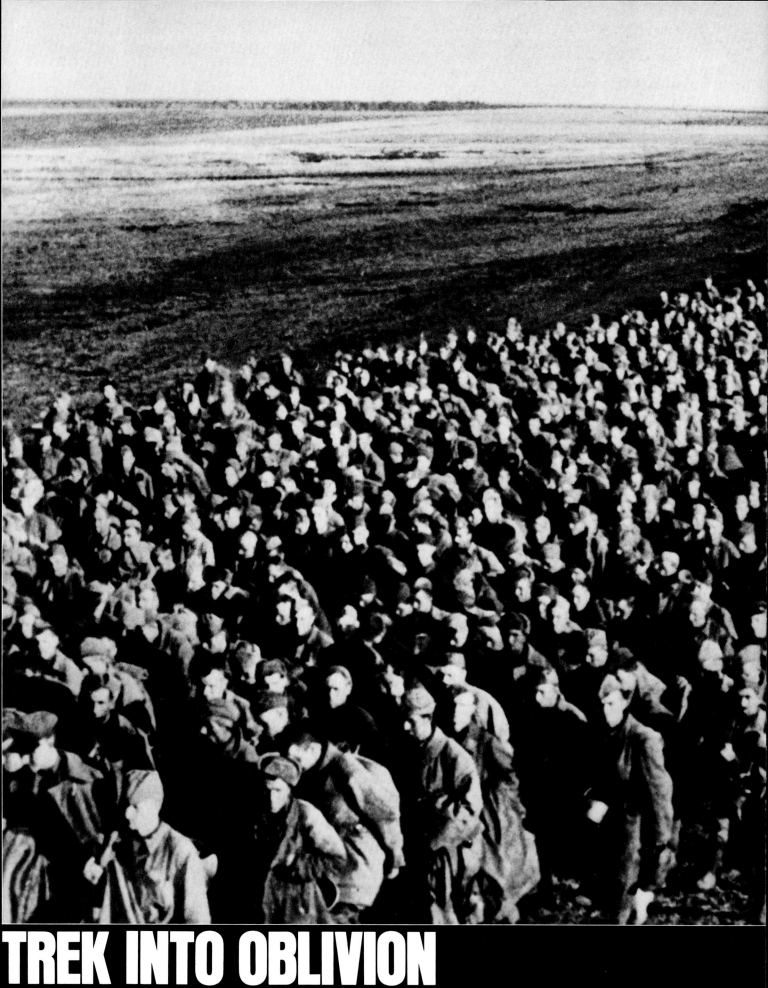

TREK INTO OBLIVION

A mass of defeated Russians straggles across a plain in 1941. In a portent of future treatment, the Germans shot many prisoners who fell along the way.

SIMPLE MECHANISMS FOR EXTERMINATION

"We used to say, 'Let's take prisoners.' Now we think 'What are we going to do with all these prisoners?'" Behind this comment by Hitler, made in October 1941—some three months following the German invasion of the Soviet Union—lay a problem of unprecedented proportions. During the summer, as German pincer movements embraced huge areas of the U.S.S.R., members of the Red Army, surrendering or defecting en masse, had poured into makeshift camps by the tens of thousands. Before the War's end, the total of Russian prisoners reached almost 5.8 million, the largest number from any single country. Two thirds of them—some 3.8 million—had been taken during the first six months after the Germans invaded.

The German solution to the problem was brutally direct. Only one major directive from Berlin dealt with prisoners. The SS was to cull out Communist Party functionaries and Jews and ship them to concentration camps for execution. The SS also formed extermination squads known as *Einsatzgruppen* (action groups) that scoured newly conquered territory and summarily killed Jews, partisans, political suspects, prisoners and other targets of opportunity.

Such Draconian policies grew out of the deep ideological hostility of the Nazis toward the Russians. The most dedicated Nazis believed that the German people had a right, based on their purported racial superiority, to carve out living space in the east. But first the land had to be depopulated for German settlement—a goal that seemed, to Nazi policymakers, to justify holding Soviet prisoners in temporary camps, with minimal food and shelter, where many would die as the winter set in.

Not all Germans approved of these measures. Army members in particular, who if captured by the Russians could expect to be treated in kind, argued for humane treatment based on such international rules as those of the Geneva Convention. Their suggestions were ignored. Before the first cruel Russian winter of the War was over, one third of the prisoners in all German-run camps—and up to 95 per cent in some—were dead.

Russian prisoners pause on the march to the rear in October of 1941. Women served in the Red Army as medical orderlies and as snipers.

Forced to march without food or water, captured Russians on their way to a German-operated prison camp gather around a hole in the ice to drink.

Holding out an array of makeshift drinking
vessels (right), Russian prisoners wait for water
to be distributed to them at a POW camp in
German-occupied Soviet territory.

Russians newly captured and suspected of being partisans dangle from gibbets that were erected for such summary hangings by roving SS death squads

When Germany invaded Poland on September 1, 1939, a 36-year-old Warsaw lawyer named Zbigniew Stypulkowski took up arms. He was issued a rifle and an Army uniform and went west to fight the invaders, but his career as a soldier was short-lived. By the end of that first month of the War, Stypulkowski was retreating eastward with the remnants of the defeated Polish Army. At that point he fell into the hands of another enemy. He became a prisoner of the Russians, who had invaded from the east on September 17 under the terms of secret arrangement with the Germans that ceded the eastern portion of Poland to the U.S.S.R.

Stypulkowski spent the next six months, cold, sick and hungry, in a series of wretched prison camps. First, he was taken to a camp 350 miles northeast of Moscow. He guessed that revealing his civilian background as a lawyer and former member of Parliament would make him dangerously vulnerable to the NKVD—the Soviet secret police—who were searching for educated Poles like himself and hustling them off to unknown destinations. His silence protected him and, after an exchange of Polish prisoners between the Russians and Germans, he was taken to a German camp in Bavaria. There he endured a month of interrogation by the Gestapo, which suspected that he was a Soviet spy. Finally, through the lucky intervention of three friendly German officers at the camp, Stypulkowski was released and sent home. In Warsaw, he became a leader of the Polish resistance movement.

Stypulkowski was one of the fortunate ones: He survived. Millions of prisoners on Europe's vast Eastern Front did not, for in that area there was no adherence to the rules of the Geneva Convention to restrain human brutality; the Soviets had not signed the Convention.

During the nearly six years of warfare in Eastern Europe, more than eight million Poles, Russians and Germans were taken prisoner. Most were confined in labor camps and set to work in mines or factories. More than five million died—starved, worn down by illness and overwork, gassed, shot or hanged. Of the Poles who survived, a handful made their way to England and joined Allied forces there. A larger contingent under General Wladyslaw Anders emerged, as a group, from confinement in the Soviet Union and fought the Germans in Italy. Some Poles, and most of the Russians and Germans, became political pawns in the mortal struggle be-

4

A pattern of abuse, manipulation and betrayal
Interrogation by brainwashing
Mass graves planted over with pine trees
"Little Stalin horses"
Gala banquets with wine and music
Special marks to identify "subhumans"
A general without an army

CHAOS ON THE EASTERN FRONT

tween Hitler and Stalin, and many were forced by circumstances—or persuaded—to turn against their homeland and even to bear arms against their fellow countrymen.

The Poles were the first to be taken prisoner, and their treatment established the pattern of abuse, manipulation and betrayal that would mark the handling of POWs on the Eastern Front throughout the War. As many as 250,000 Polish soldiers were captured by the Germans. A relatively small number of officers were held in POW camps; most of the enlisted men were turned over to the SS and enrolled in the ranks of slave laborers. Approximately 250,000 more Polish soldiers were captured by the Russians in eastern Poland and deported to the Soviet Union. Of these prisoners, the vast majority were sent to labor in far-flung penal camps where the Soviet government punished its own recalcitrant citizens.

However, certain Polish prisoners of war received singular attention. This special group comprised 15,500 POWs, including about 8,500 officers. The rest were enlisted men, noncommissioned officers and paramilitary specialists such as policemen and frontier guards. Many of them were reservists called up during Poland's last-minute mobilization. As a group, they included many of the intellectual and professional elite of their homeland. Among them were more than 1,000 lawyers, 800 doctors of medicine, numerous writers, artists, college professors, teachers and clergymen. They were, as the Polish scholar J. K. Sawodny later put it, the "brain and heart," the very "flower of Polish society."

By November 1939, two months after their conquest of eastern Poland, the Soviet authorities had divided the group among three prison camps in the western part of Russia. Each of the camps—Kozelsk, Ostashkov and Starobelsk—occupied the site of a former Russian Orthodox monastery that had been converted to the practice of high-pressure political indoctrination.

Intensive interrogation by the NKVD was the program at the three camps. The prisoners soon discovered what their interrogators were after: to identify the potential future leaders of Poland, divorce them from their national background and then convert them to the Soviet cause. A principal aim was to train a politically reliable nucleus of officers for a Polish Red Army. The Soviet techniques, which became known as brainwashing, were essentially the same as those used on U.S. prisoners of war many years later in North Korea and North Vietnam.

Interrogation often occurred in the middle of the night, and some sessions lasted for 72 hours, with Soviet agents taking turns questioning the exhausted prisoner. Agents would alternate between concern for the prisoner and insults—verbal punishment that was sometimes accompanied by beatings and other forms of torture.

One object of such treatment was to create insecurity and confusion so that the prisoner would begin to doubt his own sense of personal and cultural identity. A sensitive area for the Poles—and an important target for their Soviet warders—was organized religion. The prisoners were forbidden to engage in public prayer, and during Christmas of 1939 at Kozelsk nearly all Polish clergymen among the POWs were removed from camp.

What was most remarkable throughout this brainwashing period was the Polish will to resist. Partly because of their traditional hostility toward Russia, partly because they were highly educated and strongly patriotic, the Poles withstood the treatment meted out by the Soviets. By spring, after six months of interrogation and indoctrination, only half a dozen or so seemed ready for conversion to Marxism.

The Soviet authorities, however, had not given up hope. Beginning in March 1940, they started transferring to another camp a group of 448 prisoners—the handful of prime candidates for conversion and others whom the Communists thought might be susceptible to further persuasion. After additional indoctrination, two dozen officers from this group were personally picked by NKVD chief Lavrenty P. Beria. The selected men were sent to a special school set up in a villa in a suburb of Moscow. The house offered good food, steam heat, warm showers and two attractive young Russian chambermaids.

As a school for politically trustworthy Polish Communist officers, the villa produced only one notable alumnus. He was Zygmunt Berling, a colonel in the Polish Army. When the Soviet Union finally succeeded in forming its satellite Polish army in 1943, using POWs and conscripted Polish civilians, Berling became commander of the so-called Kościuszko Division. Ironically, the division was named for Tadeusz Kościuszko, the Polish general who had fought

In a picture shot with a camera smuggled in by a Spanish worker, Polish prisoners—still hoping to go to Britain—gather for an outdoor English class.

POLES IN A SPANISH PURGATORY

Between 1940 and 1943, some 700 Polish soldiers found themselves in neutral Spain, 1,300 miles from home. In all but name they were prisoners of war.

The routes the Poles took to reach Spain varied after their country was overrun in September 1939. Many had retreated into Hungary, which was then neutral, and had been interned. (Neutral nations may disarm and confine belligerent nations' fighting men who enter their territory.) But many of the Poles were not closely watched by their Hungarian guardians; they walked away from the internment camps and made their way to a Yugoslavian port, where they embarked for Marseilles to join the Allied forces that were fighting in France.

When France fell in June 1940, the Poles moved into Spain. They hoped that indulgent surveillance similar to that of the Hungarians would enable them to rejoin their fellow countrymen who had escaped across the English Channel from France to Britain. But as they crossed the Pyrenees, the police—Franco's Guardia Civil—handcuffed the Poles and transported them to a concentration camp in the Basque town of Miranda de Ebro.

At the camp, internees were treated as severely as Spanish prisoners. Although they were allowed to organize games and classes (above), they were fed only watery bean soup and a few ounces of bread daily. A few who attempted to escape were shot.

However, the worst problem was overcrowding. When the Germans occupied Vichy France in November 1942, an influx of refugees brought the total number of foreigners in the camp to almost 4,000 prisoners representing 32 nations.

From the beginning, the Poles were the most vocal among the non-Spanish prisoners in their protests against conditions, and the most persistent in trying to escape—attempting unsuccessfully to tunnel out five times. At the noon meal on January 6, 1943—the Feast of the Three Kings, a cherished Polish holiday—they switched tactics and started a hunger strike that by evening had been taken up by all of the other national groups. Prisoners spread word of the strike outside the camp—notably by means of a small gas-filled balloon that they made from scavenged rubber and floated over the barbed wire at night.

The hunger strike had its intended effect. It ended on the seventh day, with the arrival at the camp of the British and American Ambassadors and embarrassed Spanish authorities. The Allied landings in North Africa and Hitler's stalled advance in Russia had worked in the strikers' favor. Within a few months, all were released—and the resilient Polish soldiers went on to fight with the Allies in Western Europe.

A sentry guards a camp jail holding prisoners in solitary confinement.

Six Polish officers gather for a picture at their camp in Miranda de Ebro.

on the side of the colonists in the American Revolutionary War and later led Poland's battle for independence from Russia and Prussia.

Meanwhile, during the spring of 1940, the 15,000 prisoners who had been deemed unfit for further indoctrination were due to be moved from the three special camps. They began to sense a change when the propaganda and the all-night interrogation ceased. They heard rumors that prisoners were to be sent home in early April, and their hopes soared. Groups ranging in size from 50 to 360 men began leaving the camps by truck.

The procedures for departure followed a set pattern. At Kozelsk, for example, the routine began in the morning at about 10 o'clock, when someone in Moscow telephoned the camp commandant and gave him the list of names scheduled for departure that day. Those selected to leave were given an unusually good dinner and special travel rations—consisting of nearly two pounds of bread, some sugar and three herring.

The evacuation of Kozelsk was accomplished in 21 separate daily parties. Each group of prisoners was carried in trucks from the camp to the train station, where they were loaded into railroad cars with barred windows and locked compartments. Stanislaw Swianiewicz, who left with about 300 other prisoners on the evening of April 26, 1940, later described the journey: The Poles traveled all night northwestward, in the general direction of home. The next morning, however, the train stopped in a wooded area, known as the Katyn Forest, a few miles west of the Russian city of Smolensk. From the scribbling on his compartment wall, Swianiewicz could tell that previous groups from Kozelsk had taken the same route and stopped near Smolensk. After the train halted, an NKVD colonel who suspected Swianiewicz of espionage and wanted to question him led him out of the railroad car and took him to another one where he was locked up. "It was a fine, sunny day," Swianiewicz recalled. "The scents of spring came from the fields and, here and there, small patches of snow lay on the ground."

He watched through a window while his fellow prisoners disembarked and entered the rear of the bus backed up to the train. When it was full, the bus would drive off into the nearby woods. Half an hour or so later, it would return empty and collect another batch of prisoners. Later that day, Swianiewicz was taken to a jail in Smolensk. He assumed that the bus had transported the other prisoners to a new camp in the woods.

By early May, not only Kozelsk but also the other two special camps, Ostashkov and Starobelsk, had been emptied. For the families of the prisoners, the first indication of the move came when postcards and letters addressed to the men were sent back marked "return—gone away." Even more disturbing was the fact that though the prisoners had previously been permitted to write home once a month, all mail from them suddenly ceased. Distraught families tried without success to trace their missing men.

By the fall of 1941, the situation of most Polish POWs in Russia had changed radically. The Soviet Union, invaded by its former German ally, now needed help from its former enemy, Poland. The Soviet Union resumed diplomatic relations with the Polish government-in-exile based in London and granted amnesty to Polish POWs. Now, with Soviet help, the Poles were raising on Russian soil an exile army composed of POWs.

The commander of the new Polish army, General Anders, was a career soldier who only recently had been released from prison after withstanding 20 months of alternating physical abuse and Soviet blandishments aimed at recruiting him for the Red Army. As the emaciated Polish POWs trickled into his training centers at Buzuluk (near Kuibyshev, in eastern Russia), the general quickly became aware that many men were missing. He desperately needed officers for his army, but he could find only about 2,000. Of 14 Polish generals taken captive by the Russians, for example, only two reported. Anders began compiling lists and discovered that at least 15,000 Polish officer-prisoners were missing and unaccounted for—all from the camps at Kozelsk, Ostashkov and Starobelsk.

Messages to the underground forces in Poland turned up no traces of the missing men. Repeated inquiries to the Soviet government met with vague or evasive answers, or none at all. On December 3, 1941, Anders, along with General Wladyslaw Sikorski, the Prime Minister of the Polish government-in-exile, confronted Josef Stalin himself in Moscow about the problem. They did not get far.

"This is impossible," said Stalin of the missing 15,000. "They must have escaped."

"Where could they escape to?" asked Anders.

"Well, to Manchuria," said Stalin; he did not bother to explain how the prisoners might have made their way, undetected, 4,000 miles across the Soviet Union.

The Polish government-in-exile had promised that, when fully ready, Anders' army would fight alongside Soviet forces. But the Russian evasiveness over the missing prisoners—added to the Soviets' failure to provide adequate arms and supplies, and their constant interference with training—forced the Poles to break this commitment. In the spring of 1941, Anders' army, nearly 100,000 strong, accepted an invitation from Winston Churchill to join the British in the Middle East. These former POWs left Russia through Iran; designated the Polish II Corps, they later fought with great distinction against the Germans in Italy.

Hard facts about the fate of nearly a third of the missing Poles surfaced on April 13, 1943. The Germans, who then controlled the area around Smolensk, announced that they had found mass graves in the Katyn Forest about 10 miles west of the city. The graves, planted over with young pine trees, contained more than 4,000 corpses—the precise number is disputed. Papers found on the bodies identified them as officers and men from the camp at Kozelsk.

Each prisoner had been shot in the base of the skull by a revolver bullet of a type manufactured in Germany but exported to Poland and other Eastern European nations before the War. Many of the prisoners were bound with Russian-made rope. Some had back wounds that apparently had been caused by the Soviet Army-issue bayonet, which had distinctive grooves along the blade. According to the Germans, autopsies showed that the mass executions had occurred in the spring of 1940, when the Katyn Forest was still in Russian hands. Hence, said the Germans, the Soviet Union obviously was responsible for the killings.

Moscow called the German findings a "fabrication." Even the Poles suspected it was a German propaganda ploy. Both the Germans and the Polish government-in-exile asked the International Red Cross to send a team of investigators to the Katyn Forest; the Soviet government not only refused to approve such an investigation, but suspended diplomatic relations with the Poles. This action shocked the Poles, as

On April 21, 1943—six days after the German announcement of the discovery of mass graves of Polish officers in the Katyn Forest in Russia— a Polish Red Cross delegation watches as German soldiers exhume the bodies (top). The Germans arranged to have a Russian clergyman look on as medical examiners performed an autopsy (bottom). When the Russians recaptured the area five months later, they contended that the officers had been killed by Germans during their two-year occupation.

did the new Russian account of what had happened to the Kozelsk prisoners. These prisoners, said the Soviet government, had been building roads near Smolensk during the summer of 1941 and had fallen into German hands.

Two weeks after the announcement of the graves' discovery, the Germans proceeded to clinch their case against the Russians. They brought to the Katyn Forest an international commission of 12 specialists in forensic medicine, which deals with the medical aspects of criminal law; a delegation from the Polish Red Cross; and Western Allied POWs, including Lieut. Colonel Donald B. Stewart and Lieut. Colonel John H. van Vliet Jr., U.S. Army officers who had been captured in North Africa. Eleven of the medical specialists, from German-occupied Europe, may have been pro-Nazi, but the 12th, from neutral Switzerland, was known to be anti-Nazi. The Red Cross medical team was from German-occupied Poland; its Nazi hosts were unaware that it included several members of the underground.

The international commission and the Poles, after independently examining a number of corpses, confirmed the essential points of the earlier German findings. The prisoners had been dead about three years, a conclusion borne out by the growth rings in trees planted over the graves.

Colonel van Vliet later stated that he had resisted believing anything the Germans told him about the killings; but both he and Colonel Stewart could easily see that the corpses' clothing and footgear were in good repair. Their own experience as POWs told them that shoes and uniforms could not have remained in such condition if the men had worn them in a prison camp and on work details during the year or so between spring 1940 and summer 1941, as the Russians claimed. Distasteful though it was for them to exonerate the Germans, both officers could only conclude that the Russians were guilty. They refused, however, to reveal their opinions until after the War.

After the Red Army recaptured the Katyn Forest in September 1943, the Soviet government sent its own medical experts to examine the graves. Significantly, this was an all-Russian team; even Polish Communists were barred from participation. In the graves, the Russian investigators purported to find nine documents, mostly newspaper clippings, dated after the Germans took over the area. From this evidence, the Russians concluded that the prisoners had been executed by the German Army late in the summer of 1941.

To publicize their claim, the Russians took a group of Western correspondents based in Moscow to the Katyn graves. Kathleen Harriman—the 25-year-old daughter of W. Averell Harriman, the U.S. Ambassador to the Soviet Union and a Moscow representative of the U.S. Office of War Information—was included in the group at the Ambassador's request. When she asked why the dead Poles were wearing greatcoats and winter underwear if they were killed in the summer, a Russian spokesman replied that it must have been a cold summer. (In fact, the mean temperature around Smolensk in August and September is 65° F.)

Despite private misgivings, Miss Harriman retailed the Soviets' story as they had presented it. So did the U.S. and British governments—at least in their official pronouncements. Neither Winston Churchill nor Franklin Roosevelt wanted to ruffle the feathers of their Soviet allies.

But the Soviet version would not wash. At the postwar Nuremberg trials, a Russian attempt to blame the Katyn murders on the Germans failed. In 1952, amid strong anti-Communist feeling at the height of the Korean War, a U.S. Congressional investigating committee was established to fix the blame for the massacre. On the basis of testimony from such witnesses as van Vliet and Stewart, the committee concluded that the Soviet government was responsible, "beyond any question of reasonable doubt." The fate of the other 10,000 Polish prisoners, those taken from the camps at Ostashkov and Starobelsk during the spring of 1940, remains a mystery. Presumably they died in mass executions like those in the Katyn Forest.

Mass executions were actually the exception in the standard Soviet treatment of POWs, notably the more than three million German military men who fell into their hands during

In a clandestine photograph taken in September 1945, German POW laborers haul a heavy cart of wood across a field near Koksyltau in the U.S.S.R. While one prisoner guided the cart by its shafts, the others worked in pairs in an arrangement the prisoners themselves devised to prevent some men from dawdling while others did the work. Each pair was connected to the cart by a separate rope tied to the middle of a stick. If one man pulled harder, the stick pivoted, exposing the slacker.

the War. Unprotected by the Geneva Convention, the Germans in Russian captivity seldom had enough to eat or adequate means to ward off the epidemics of typhus and typhoid that swept their camps periodically. A cruel work-incentive plan prevailed in those camps. Norms for work production were set; theoretically, if a prisoner could exceed the norm, he received extra rations. But the catch was grim: A prisoner who attempted to beat the quota often was trapped in a self-defeating circle; he would drive himself to the limit of his endurance for a day or so—but fall short on succeeding days and then receive even less to eat than he had been given before.

One of the worst jobs in the camps was getting in wood during the winter. Dressed in rags and thin boots, and working without gloves, a team of four prisoners assigned to the task had to cut, split and pile the day's quota of 864 cubic feet of wood—almost seven cords. Other prisoners, harnessed by ropes to sledges and carts, hauled in the cut timber; they were nicknamed "little Stalin horses" by the Russians. In such conditions it is not surprising that of the estimated 3.5 million Germans taken captive by the Russians in four years of war, 1.5 million did not survive.

The Russians, who were eager to recruit propagandists from among the German prisoners to wage psychological warfare against their countrymen, did offer one way to escape death in camps: submission to indoctrination. Looking a long way ahead, the Russians were laying the groundwork for a pro-Soviet government to replace the Nazis in Germany after the War. Soviet indoctrination efforts focused upon exploiting the grievances of German enlisted men and noncommissioned officers in order to isolate soldiers from their commanders. In October 1941, only three months after the Germans invaded the U.S.S.R., the Russians stage-managed the First Conference of German Prisoners, a propaganda session where 158 carefully selected soldiers were encouraged to vent their hostility toward German officers.

But these outpourings were merely a kind of scene-setter. The real effort was directed toward finding leaders. The Russians were actively seeking out German officers—particularly those who were strongly nationalistic but did not like Hitler. Within the year, the Russians had an important catch: Lieutenant Heinrich von Einsiedel, a 21-year-old Luftwaffe fighter pilot with 35 Soviet planes to his credit, who was shot down on August 30, 1942, during the early stages of the Battle of Stalingrad. Einsiedel was the great-grandson of Otto von Bismarck, the 19th Century statesman and first Chancellor of modern Germany. A staunch German patriot who hated Hitler, the young nobleman was ripe for Soviet indoctrination. Living in the Third Reich, he wrote later, produced "a kind of split consciousness that was typical not only of my family but of large middle-class groups in Germany. We despised the Nazis and yet served them because they represented the power of Germany."

Einsiedel's captors had little trouble persuading him to talk about his doubts that Germany could win the War. Within a few days, he had put those doubts into writing for use in propaganda leaflets to be dropped over the German lines around Stalingrad. Soon Einsiedel was attending one of the "anti-Fascist" schools set up especially for promising German prisoners and was becoming steeped in the writings of Marx and Lenin. Marxism, he decided, would provide a means of healing his "split consciousness."

Einsiedel was a fast learner. After a few months of study, on July 12, 1943, he helped organize the Free Germany Committee, the principal Soviet mechanism for employing prisoners as propagandists. The committee included not only converted POWs, but also old-line German Communists who had emigrated to the Soviet Union after Hitler came to power in 1932. One of the committee's members was Walter Ulbricht, the stern émigré who would become the postwar leader of Communist East Germany.

Under the auspices of the committee, the Soviets formed a second POW organization, the League of German Officers. The league included several generals who had been among the 90,000 Germans captured at Stalingrad in the winter of 1942-1943. These officers were not necessarily

converts to Communism. But they feared for the future of their country and hoped to secure places for themselves in postwar Germany. After the debacle at Stalingrad, from which the Führer would permit no retreat, the German officers could rationalize their own treason by insisting that Hitler was the traitor, betraying loyal Germans like themselves by leading the nation down the path of destruction.

Besides allaying fears for the future, membership in the league offered some immediate amenities: decent housing, some freedom to move about, better rations than the Red Army received, and even gala banquets with copious wine and liquor, cigarettes, and music by a POW orchestra—always, of course, under NKVD supervision.

The German officers did not actually have to fight their countrymen in return for such treatment. They were asked only to help win them over. The officers talked to Germany daily over Moscow radio and produced a weekly newspaper called *Freies Deutschland (Free Germany)*, which was air-dropped over the German lines by the hundreds of thousands. The league officers went to the front lines and broadcast loudspeaker messages urging their fellow Germans to organize for the overthrow of Hitler.

"The reactions to these speeches were extremely varied," wrote Einsiedel. "In many places the front sank into deep silence, listening. We had suggested the soldiers fire three shots into the air in token of agreement—they did it! On the other hand, in certain units angry machine-gun and hand-grenade fire was the reply, and sometimes even the artillery took part in these attempts to silence us. Occasionally assault groups were sent to wipe us out."

Whatever the immediate reaction, the overall effect of this propaganda barrage was probably minimal. But as the Red Army went on the offensive and more and more Germans fell into Russian hands, top-ranking prisoners flocked to join the league. By February 1945, no fewer than 50 captive German generals were signing or broadcasting appeals to their countrymen to give up the battle. One of them was the German commander at the Battle of Stalingrad, Field Marshal Friedrich von Paulus.

An even more remarkable turnabout was occurring on the other side of the Eastern Front: Hundreds of thousands of Russians, prisoners of the Germans, were bearing arms

Lieutenant Heinrich von Einsiedel (far left), a grandson of Otto von Bismarck—Germany's 19th Century unifier—was a famous participant at a 1943 meeting in Moscow of a Soviet-sponsored group that was formed to attempt to turn German soldiers in Russia against Hitler.

The Illustrated Front, a slick propaganda paper dropped by Russian planes, tries to lure German soldiers into defecting by telling them, in the legend at top, that their captured comrades "live better in Russian camps and are better fed than their families in Germany." The picture at upper left purports to show a German field commander (rear) chatting amicably with a Russian commissar; the other pictures advertise the tender treatment awaiting wounded prisoners of war.

Army ju
brutality
harshnes
was one
gime. Inc
governm
Kremlin
through
faith. The
taminate
Soviet U
oners we
arch emb
Its Heroe
shipped c

The rej
effort to e
posed to
their resp
parcels. "
in turning
till death.
matically

against
Russiar
vasion
sponse
a desir
the end
ing occ
spite Hi
man ma
Ukraini

The c
Russian
man Arr
clothing
against
identity
of its ow

As pr
that Sla
the fact
ler's ant
statistics
en prisor

Possib
ciplinary
political
stereotyp
it, a pris
read or
that the
extermin
Zyklon B
The rest
ease and

In the
that they
of prison
taken pri:
invasion.
sisted on
great Ger
such cent

During

SPINNING PROPAGANDA
OUT OF BROKEN PRIDE

Propaganda Russians took their first significant haul of German prisoners at Stalingrad in February 1943, propagandists seized the opportunity to explode the myth of German military superiority. Far from being goose-stepping supermen, the 91,000 members of the Sixth Army captured at Stalingrad were sick, starving and often half-demented from the long siege. When pictures of them were prominently displayed in newsreels and posters, the average Soviet citizen reveled in their misery. It seemed incredible that the Germans, with their reputation for efficiency, had been so illprepared for the notorious chill—often as low as −40° F.—of the Russian winter.

The best use of German prisoners as a propaganda tool came in the summer of 1944. During a gigantic Red Army offensive timed to coincide with the June landings of the Western Allies in Normandy, nearly 85,000 Germans fell into Russian hands as the German Army Group Center was smashed in Belorussia. For Stalin and his propaganda team, the plethora of prisoners offered rich opportunities. Not only would the POWs bring home to the Russian people the magnitude of the Soviet victory, but they could also be used to refute the evidence claims by the Germans that in pulling back they were simply staging a planned withdrawal in the East. The large numbers of captives also undercut insinuations in the Western press that the Red Army was advancing so quickly only because German troops had been diverted to the new Western Front.

To concentrate the impact of their demonstration, the Soviets stuffed many of the prisoners into boxcars and took them to Moscow. On July 17, 1944, in a carefully staged spectacle (pages 134-135) that brought to mind the ancient Roman custom of parading captives in triumph, some 57,000 tired and filthy German prisoners were marched through the Russian capital with their generals in the lead. The crowds looked on in astonishment, wrote one German marcher, at the wretched remnants of the formerly unbeatable, always victorious German Wehrmacht which now trudged by so ragged and defeated.

High-ranking officers captured at Stalingrad in 1943, still exude arrogance with their posture, ribbons and medals, stand in a prison camp.

PORTRAIT OF THE FOE
A MOB OF OLD MEN

With reference to portraying "Fritz" —the pejorative German epithet for a German soldier— Russians took great delight in accentuating the photographic disparity between ... the various ... Defeated men the Red Army captured in pictures such as the ... Soviet photojournal... singled out subjects who ... and haggard.

Ironically, as Germany began to collapse ... cameras were focused ... on the aged men that the desperate ... had sent into battle. ... the picture conveyed to the Soviet Union—and the world—was ... Fritz was a fearsome ... longer, but instead a shivering ...

German prisoners ... hang dejectedly in defeat ... in the summer of 1944 ... fighting camp outside Moscow ... in retaliation.

After being taken prisoner in 1945 by Russian troops advancing on Berlin, a man apparently wearing military age stares fearfully into the camera. Like other conscripts hastily put in defense of home territory, the man and his companions were members of the Volkssturm, or home guard, which pressed into duty under 16 and men aged 16 to 70.

Another prisoner in the ragged remains of a coat taken at Stalingrad in 1943 conscript, his head covered with a ragged blanket. The Stalingrad defenders, exiled to labor in the harsh conditions in Russia, learned to improvise against the cold with strips of clothing—and such other.

A CHANCE TO VILIFY
THE FORMER CONQUERORS

Whether they were seen in the flesh or in
news pictures, the long lines of German
captives being led to prison camps provided a badly needed boost in morale for
Russian civilians and soldiers alike. After
the years of brutal German occupation,
Soviet propagandists played on the Russian people's desire for retribution. Posters
blatantly advised Russian soldiers advancing on Germany that the hour of revenge
had struck. Similarly, on the home
front, photographs like this one were published showing a woman jeering at German prisoners of war.

In mid-April 1945, however, there was
an abrupt about-face in the Soviet line as
Stalin proclaimed that "Hitlers come and
go, but the German people go on forever."
The shrewd Soviet leader did not want to
let an orgy of revenge on surrendering soldiers and civilians undermine his plan to
set up a docile, industrially productive satellite in the portion of Germany allotted to
him for postwar occupation.

In any event, the propaganda did not always work. Some Russians displayed an
unexpected sympathy for the fallen Germans. Watching the 1944 parade of German prisoners in Moscow, one old woman
was overheard murmuring, "Just like our
poor boys . . . also driven into the War."

114

AN EASYGOING CUSTODY

In a camp in Tennessee, German prisoners of war salute the official German Army flag, a privilege granted to them by the U.S. Army throughout the War.

ACCOMMODATIONS ON THE GI PLAN

While keeping a careful eye on Geneva Convention rules, the Army built prison camps in the United States as economically as possible. Materials were utilitarian: pine lumber, tar paper and concrete. To conserve heating fuel, the Army located many camps in southern states, where the climate was uncomfortable for most Europeans. A new arrival in the Southwest wrote home: "The heat is so intense one dares not venture outside."

For all their drabness and despite their location, the camps impressed most prisoners. Amenities that were considered luxurious in the camps of their own armed forces—among them modern plumbing and well-stocked canteens—were commonplace in American POW compounds. A comment by a prisoner in Camp Trinidad, Colorado, was typical: "I have never as a soldier been as well off as I am here; we are being treated much better than we were by our own officers." An Afrika Korps veteran struck an arrogant note in comments about the good treatment, telling an interpreter, "When Germany wins the War, this will make at least one good point in your favor."

A wide, unpaved street separates rows of tar-paper prison barracks at Camp Polk, near Leesville, Louisiana—a camp that housed American GIs as well as prisoners of war.

Prisoners in an enlisted men's compound at Camp Blanding, Florida, relax in GI comfort: Army cots, magazines and a wall that is covered with pinups of American movie stars.

Two officer-prisoners admire the same pinups as those available to the enlisted men, but enjoy them in more comfortable quarters—rank's privilege even in captivity.

IN PURSUIT OF PLEASURE

In the evening and on days off from work, POWs in American camps were free to engage in a wide range of activities. Prisoner orchestras performed at concerts and dances, where men danced together. At the camp in Aliceville, Alabama, prisoners maintained a garden of topiary, or sculpted shrubs. Prisoners at Camp Shelby, Mississippi, caught water moccasins and used the snakeskins to make souvenirs, which they sold to the guards. Artists painted landscapes, still lifes and, from memory, battlefield scenes for exhibitions that were community events in Fort Du Pont, Delaware, and Camp Como, Mississippi.

Resourceful prisoners at Camp Crowder, Missouri, established a zoo, complete with an aviary containing parrots, lovebirds and quail. The animals included alligators, monkeys, white mice and a pig.

Sports were the most popular pastime, but the American football that guards attempted to teach the prisoners was not a success—when the ball was snapped, both teams converged on the ball-carrier. Soccer teams drew ardent fans in every compound and attracted some American supporters. Civilians from Atlanta, Nebraska, pulled off U.S. Route 6 to look at matches through the wire at the nearby camp. At Opelika, Alabama, guards applauded their favorite soccer teams from the watchtowers, and when off duty, they brought their families to the games.

POW spectators watch intently as two of their soccer teams do battle; injured knees were a frequent complaint in the hospitals at prisoner-of-war camps.

REPLACING ABSENT LABOR WITH PRISONERS

Two million Americans were serving overseas by June 1943; millions of others supported them at home in war-related industry. As a result, a perilous manpower shortage developed in the less-essential sectors of the American economy at the same time that the prisoner-of-war population in the United States began to swell—from 53,000 to 163,000 by September 1943, and to more than double that number by the end of the War.

The Army put prisoners to work at military bases, farms, and in such industries as food processing, logging and mining; but some of the Americans thus benefited were less than grateful. A Huntsville, Texas, farmer was disgusted when the Germans sent to work for him turned out not to know "a stalk of cotton from a goddamn cocklebur." Envious timber workers in Duluth, Minnesota, raged over the bathing facilities and electric lights planned for a prison lumberjacking camp in their area.

But most Americans liked the POW laborers. Farmers described them as generally cooperative, well-mannered, intelligent and good-natured. A Texan working alongside the prisoners said, "It's a pity that nice young folks like them should get in so much devilment that they have to chop cotton so far from home."

In their turn, prisoners welcomed the opportunity to get out of camp and to earn wages—of 80 cents a day.

A rancher near Camp McAlester, Oklahoma, found the chief difficulty in the POW work program was "having to show them, instead of telling them what to do." But he agreed with others who employed prisoners: "They've been our salvation."

*Prisoners mend uniforms at Fort Meade,
Maryland; a sign above them lists the English
and German words for parts of garments.*

Watched by a guard, two prisoners use a mule-drawn plow and a rake to cultivate a Tennessee farmer's cornfield, near the POW camp at Crossville.

Three Afrika Korps veterans belly up to a camp canteen bar in Aliceville, Alabama, to sample an American staple: Coca-Cola. At some camps POWs could also buy beer and wine at the commandant's discretion.

Coupons redeemable at the canteen served as POWs' wages under terms of the Geneva Convention.

A prisoner stocks canteen shelves with American toiletries, candy and cigarettes. Goods ranging from cameras to cigarette lighters were also available.

A German officer buys a carton of cigarettes at a canteen manned by a fellow prisoner. Prices were approximately the same as those paid by American GIs.

Two POW cooks report to a German mess sergeant. Germans baked home-style black bread and American-inspired white bread.

SEATS AT THE GROANING AMERICAN BOARD

At American camps, the food was so good and so plentiful that one German refrained from writing home about it, fearing that his letters would be used for American propaganda. Another prisoner did write home, declaring the food better than what he remembered from German Army life: "Here we eat more in a single day than we did during a whole week."

Using abundant meat and vegetables, prisoner-of-war cooks brought to the cuisine of their camps a European flavor that was a revelation for many Americans. One guard commented, "It looks like these foreigners take their cooking more seriously than we do."

As long as food costs equaled those for American troops, POW menus could include ethnic ingredients—pig's knuckles and wurst, for example. And true to European tradition, scraps and bones went into soups and stews. As a result, at Camp McAlester the garbage collector canceled his contract because the size of his load did not justify the cost of his trip.

Christmas dinner, 1943, Camp Swift, Texas: The original picture caption noted that POWs ate the same "luxurious fare" as the 90,000 GIs stationed there.

A Nazi flag drapes the coffin at the funeral of a prisoner of war in the Army Chapel at Fort Custer, Michigan. At the graveside of a comrade who died of

illness in the post hospital at Jefferson Barracks, St. Louis, Missouri, in the autumn of 1944, German prisoners raise their arms in a Nazi Party salute (inset).

States, authorities recorded 2,827 individual escape attempts—2,222 German, 604 Italian and one Japanese.

The growing need for hands and strong backs led to expansion of the work program in the face of opposition from jittery prison authorities. During the summer of 1943, after months of debate within the government, prisoners were made available as contract labor for civilian projects away from military installations. The debate had focused not only on security but also on War Department concerns about adhering to the Geneva Convention in matters of work assigned to prisoners, and American trade union concerns that POW laborers might displace American workers. Those worries were outweighed by the fact that the United States was facing a critical manpower shortage.

Nonetheless, the final go-ahead on using prisoners in civilian jobs was tightly constrained by red tape. To mollify the unions, employers had to show that no Americans were available to do the work. To keep POW labor competitive, employers had to pay the U.S. government, as the contractor, the local prevailing wage for the job. They also had to agree to hire at least 15 prisoners for a given project. To satisfy the Geneva Convention, employers were required to certify that the work was safe and within the prisoner's capacity; no prisoner could be required to work more than 10 hours a day, including travel time to and from camp, nor more than six days a week. Most important, under the Convention, prisoners could not be hired for work directly related to the war. That rule went through various interpretations, and the U.S. government eventually approved putting POWs to work on a jeep assembly line, explaining that the vehicles being built were destined for noncombat use only.

As the labor program grew, prisoners cut timber, canned food and worked in foundries and open-pit mines; before the Nazi extermination of Jews became widely known, German POWs even packed meat at a kosher plant in New Jersey. Most commonly, in practically every state, prisoners worked on farms. They dug peanuts in Georgia and potatoes in Maine, picked tomatoes in Indiana and cotton in Texas. With the help of an illustrated leaflet, "Snap Sweet Corn Easier and Faster," that was translated into German, they gathered corn in Illinois. In 1944 alone, prisoners harvested more than 246,000 acres of sugar cane in Louisiana.

The POW work force consisted primarily of low-ranking enlisted men—privates and corporals, and their equivalents in the Axis navies and the German secret police, the SS. To make sure the men worked, the War Department got as tough as it ever did with prisoners: By June 1943 authorities laid down a policy of "no work, no eat." Malingerers would be placed on a daily diet of 18 ounces of bread and all the water they wanted, and would have part of their canteen allowance and pay for past work withheld.

But stern measures were seldom necessary. The Nazi government—communicating through the Red Cross—encouraged German prisoners in the United States to work, fearing that widespread malingering might be emulated by American prisoners badly needed as laborers in Germany. The prisoners themselves, if not eager to work, at least were generally willing. Work was a way to break the monotony of confinement, learn about America, save a little money and meet civilians, including women. By 1945, more than 95 per cent of the POWs in the United States who were eligible under the Geneva Convention were working.

Though officers could not be forced to work, and noncommissioned officers were required only to act as supervisors, substantial numbers from these ranks volunteered for the job program—7 per cent of the officers and 45 per cent of the NCOs. In addition to military pay of 10 cents a day, POW workers received wages of 80 cents a day (50 cents in Canada), compensation based on the pay of a U.S. Army private in 1941, which was $21 a month. Exceptional performance merited a bonus of up to 40 cents a day. All wages and bonuses were paid in canteen coupons.

In San Francisco Bay, Japanese prisoners sit belowdecks on a harbor boat taking them off the transport that brought them to the United States. They were already wearing the "PW"-marked garb issued at a prisoner processing center in the Pacific. Next stop: processing at a nearby base before being sent to a camp inland. Most of the 5,200 Japanese imprisoned in the United States were held in Wisconsin and Iowa.

For the most part, the prisoners were efficient and industrious workers, though they never did learn to pick cotton properly. They got on well with their civilian employers, especially farm families. Near Peabody, Kansas, farmers' wives who mended the clothing of their POW workers and baked them cakes and cookies had to be cautioned by camp authorities against undue fraternization.

After Italy's capitulation in 1943, Italian workers presented a special problem of wartime politics. Under their ambiguous status of cobelligerency, most of the approximately 50,000 Italian POWs in the United States were organized into so-called Italian Service Units. No longer technically POWs but still far from free to do as they pleased, they were given standard military job instruction for eight to 12 weeks (skipping combat exercises and weapons training), and assigned to war-related jobs primarily in the Army Transportation, Quartermaster and Ordnance Corps. They received a third of their wages in U.S. currency, which they could spend in their comparative "liberty" off their military bases: Every three months they could leave the base in groups of 10 to 25, accompanied by an unarmed Army escort. This freedom, especially when it involved mixing with young American women at dances, often irked U.S. servicemen and civilians who had a difficult time drawing the fine legal line between a cobelligerent and a prisoner of war.

As the work program proved its worth, concerns about security dwindled. Early in 1944, the U.S. War Department adopted a policy of "calculated risk." Increasingly, POW

workers were detached from their bases and housed in lightly guarded satellite, or branch, camps situated near their jobs. And though Army regulations initially required one guard for every 10 prisoners on the job, in time it was not unusual to see one guard supervising a cotton field where 80 or 90 prisoners were working. On occasion, the guards disappeared completely. Two Alabama highway patrolmen were astonished when they stopped a car for speeding and found it loaded with German prisoners, who were on an errand for their farmer employer.

With most problems formerly regarded as serious now resolved, the POW work program displayed some obvious plusses and only a few minuses. Besides releasing American civilians for more essential war work and permitting more GIs to be sent overseas, the program had one unexpected benefit: It turned a profit for the U.S. government. In all, the government realized an estimated $230 million profit from prisoner-of-war labor. This took into account work performed on military installations as well as the hefty share of the prisoners' wages that the government collected by contracting POW labor to civilians: After deducting 80 cents a day to cover the compensation allocated to each prisoner, the government kept the remainder of the wage paid by the employer. The profits helped finance the care of the prisoners.

The work program was also popular with the public and with business, though there were occasional problems with labor unions such as Local 56 of the Amalgamated Meat Cutters and Butcher Workmen, which wanted to deduct union dues from the wages of 165 POWs employed by Seabrook Farms, a food processing concern in Bridgeton, New Jersey. POW workers became such an integral element of the national economy that in February 1945, Congressional pressure forced the War Department to rescind a decision made late in 1944 to cut off the flow of prisoners to the United States. Even after the War, further pressure from business and farm groups successfully delayed the return of the German POWs to Europe. (Italians, by virtue of their cobelligerent status, had already started the journey home.)

Canada had no work program for POWs during the first three years it operated camps, most of which were in Ontario. The Canadians attempted a volunteer working arrangement during 1943, with only a small percentage of the Ger-

mans participating. The pay—50 cents a day—was no real incentive, especially to Afrika Korps veterans who were not keen on aiding their enemies. In August of 1944, in time for the grain harvest, the Canadians made the work program mandatory. Altogether 18,000 prisoners were put to work, primarily as lumberjacks in the Ontario forests, and as agricultural laborers in Alberta and Saskatchewan. Once actively involved, the Germans adapted quickly and worked hard, reacting favorably to their open-air life and, above all, to removal from their fenced prison compounds.

The work program proved valuable for Canada, as it had for America and Great Britain. So many agricultural workers had gone into uniform or moved to war industries that authorities feared food production in the 1944 harvest would be drastically curtailed. But in two fertile—though scantily populated—areas of Alberta, the POW work force averted major crop losses, and in most areas the harvests actually increased as a result of the prisoners' labor.

In Britain, German POW labor was not used until late in 1944, when the need for their hands became urgent enough to justify bringing large numbers of them into the United Kingdom. A serious problem, as they started to enter the country, was a lack of accommodations. Camps were hurriedly built while thousands of German POWs waited in Belgium to be sent across the Channel.

British farmers and other employers were initially wary of the Germans entering the work force in 1944; the effectiveness of the POWs was limited because they worked in large, heavily guarded gangs. But the demands of the 1944 harvest required the use of smaller, unescorted groups. To accomplish this, the British tried to separate those prisoners who were willing to work from the Nazi camp leaders; Nazi leaders discouraged work volunteers. The British screened the prisoners and established a few segregated camps according to degrees of political malleability. Nazi prisoners were classified as "blacks," anti-Nazis were "whites," and all those in between—the majority—were "grays." The whites and most of the grays were successfully put to work; the blacks were used in limited ways.

Such ideological screening and segregation of Germans were not, at first, part of the American prisoner-of-war program. Because of the isolation of the U.S. camps and the ab-

sence of work programs initially, there seemed little point. As a result, the hardened Nazis who could be found in all the camps were barely identified, let alone segregated, and they represented a potential for tension and violence.

Such an arrangement was a recipe for trouble. Behind the positive image of German prisoners trustworthy enough to work outside the camps lay the darker picture of Nazi terrorism and control within the camps. From the outset, the hardened Nazis among the prisoners took over the positions of authority in the POW hierarchy. Nazis got themselves elected camp spokesmen, responsible for dealing with the U.S. authorities, and made such key decisions as selecting movies for the prisoners and choosing the curricula for camp classes. Considering themselves still at war, they took pains to stir up trouble—just as the Allied prisoners were doing in Germany. But there was more violence in the American camps: sit-down strikes, threats against fellow prisoners, and even beatings and murders.

Behind the American failure to prevent these abuses by segregating the Nazis lay a misconception of Germany and Nazism. At first the Army assumed that virtually all German prisoners were true believers in Nazism and that the few anti-Nazis would thus be prominent and easily identifiable. In February 1943, expecting anti-Nazis to be in the minority, the Army ordered camp commanders to ship apparently anti-Nazi prisoners to one of three special camps being established for their protection.

However, within five months the authorities realized that the majority of prisoners were not truly Nazis—though they often were unwilling or afraid to speak out. Consequently, the War Department reversed its policy, establishing a special camp at Alva, Oklahoma, for men that it described as "Nazi leaders, Gestapo agents and extremists."

To a flawed policy, the Army added inadequate follow-through—and another deficiency was revealed. Lacking clear guidelines for defining Nazis, camp commanders tended to send to Alva anyone who proved troublesome, regardless of his political bent. This led the War Department to warn camp administrators that "certain symptoms of barbed-wire psychosis such as suspicion, distrust, bumptiousness and irritability growing out of concern for friends, relatives and conditions in Germany . . . should not be mistaken for symptoms of Nazi convictions or affiliations."

In truth, the situation within the camps was more complex. According to various surveys, no more than 10 per cent of German POWs were ardent believers in Nazism, but an additional 30 per cent were sympathetic to the party. Furthermore, all members of the German armed forces had sworn an oath of allegiance to the Führer.

Nazi domination of the U.S. camps was strengthened by laxity in enforcing rules against guards' fraternization with POWs, and by the caliber of guards and officers themselves. Many of the guards were raw recruits or men deemed physically or psychologically unfit for combat; others were soldiers who had been wounded in battle and who shared a common bond of combat experience with the Germans.

Influenced by the POWs, many guards developed an undue admiration for the Germans' discipline. The recollections of American guards commonly reflected Sergeant Richard Staff's attitude about his German charges: "Damn!

They were a well-disciplined bunch of guys—physically healthy, well-trained and excellent soldiers. They still maintained the dignity and discipline that they had learned in the German Army, and I—we all—respected them." (But one guard went to the opposite extreme; explaining afterward that he hated Germans, one night he methodically poured 30-caliber machine-gun fire into rows of tents at a temporary camp in Utah, killing eight sleeping prisoners and wounding 20. After the guard was arrested, an examination of his records revealed that he had a history of emotional problems.)

For guards and prisoners alike, language problems complicated everything. Camp garrisons suffered from a lack of interpreters; some camps of up to 10,000 prisoners had only a single staff interpreter. This created embarrassing incidents: At Camp Breckinridge, Kentucky, for example, the camp commander personally led a procession of several

AN ODDBALL CASE OF TREASON

Growing up lonely in the 1930s, a whiz at languages—especially German—in college, Dale Maple was a youthful military enthusiast and an early Nazi sympathizer. He was a private first class in the U.S. Army when he helped a pair of German prisoners of war try to escape from a compound at Camp Hale, Colorado, on February 15, 1943. For this act, Maple became the first native-born American soldier ever convicted of treason—and perhaps the oddest figure in the story of Axis prisoners in the United States.

As a youngster in San Diego, Maple—described by a high-school classmate as a "queer, pale, ugly duckling and a sissy"—had few friends. But he was a musical prodigy with an I.Q. higher than 150, and he won a scholarship to Harvard University. There Maple carved a reputation as a linguist; among other things he spoke German like a native.

A member of the Army's Reserve Officers Training Corps in high school and college, Maple became increasingly attracted to Nazi ideology. He graduated from Harvard in 1941, and after Pearl Har-

bor he joined the U.S. Army and served an uneventful year's hitch as a radio operator. When the Army caught up with his pro-Nazi past, however, he was transferred to a special unarmed labor unit set up for men—mostly native Germans and Italians—considered poor security risks, and in 1943 he was stationed at Camp Hale.

At last Maple found friends—not only in his new Army unit but also in a totally unexpected quarter: among German prisoners who were confined in a segregated enclosure at Camp Hale. On one three-day pass, Maple sneaked into the POW compound and spent his entire leave hobnobbing with his POW comrades.

Later, he returned their friendship by helping two of them in an abortive attempt to escape to Mexico. When he was caught and court-martialed, Maple's defense was bizarre: He claimed that he had only intended to shock the authorities into acknowledging that the existence of his unit was a discredit to America. Unimpressed, the court found Maple guilty of treason, and he spent seven years in the federal penitentiary at Fort Leavenworth, Kansas.

Photographed while he was awaiting trial for masterminding the escape of two German prisoners of war, Army PFC Dale Maple wears a uniform salvaged from prewar supplies and issued to his unit of security risks.

hundred prisoners to church one Sunday morning, blissfully unaware that the march they were lustily singing was "Horst Wessel," a provocative Nazi anthem.

The official interpretation of the Geneva Convention added to the problem. The Convention permitted the wearing of decoration and insignia; U.S. authorities went so far as to allow the display of Hitler's picture on barracks walls. (This was a practice the British never allowed. The British War Office dryly commented: "There is no record of the display in a camp in Germany or Italy of portraits of His Majesty the King or the Prime Minister.") At Fort Lewis, Washington, POWs celebrated the Führer's birthday by running the swastika up the stockade flagpole.

Perhaps the most blatant symbol of the Nazi victory over American naïveté was that, from the beginning, some camp leaders accepted the Hitler salute—because the Geneva Convention requires that captors be saluted by POWs in the manner prescribed by their army. In fact, the German Army did not adopt the Hitler salute until July 1944. Earlier, German soldiers used the universal military salute—the hand brought to the cap visor—everywhere except in certain American camps. There the Nazi leaders, with U.S. acquiescence, required that POWs raise the right arm, keep the palm of the hand downward, and shout "Heil Hitler."

The Nazis tried to extend their influence not only within individual camps, but into an intercamp network. For a period in 1944, they succeeded by manipulating the POW postal system. More than 200 German noncommissioned officers who had refused to do farm work were assigned to handle POW mail at the central military post office for the American Southwest at Camp Hearne, Texas. The Germans, many of them Nazis, had access to official directories listing all prisoners in the United States; from these they compiled a blacklist of men suspected of having anti-Nazi political leanings before Hitler came to power. Then, by adding messages to mail after the U.S. authorities had censored it, and by illegally sending their own uncensored letters to various camps, they passed the word to fellow Nazis who were imprisoned with the "traitors."

In some places, the *Lagergestapo*—the prisoners' secret police—was already keeping close watch on those suspected of insufficient allegiance to Hitler. Often, suspicion led to drastic measures—direct or indirect. A suggestion that the War was going badly, or even church attendance, might bring threats of reprisal after the War. More immediate retribution usually took the form of a beating; beatings were reported in nearly 200 camps. At Camp Concordia, Kansas, physical intimidation was so commonplace that many prisoners kept clubs by their beds for self-protection.

The terror reached a bloody peak between September 1943 and April 1944. During this period, there were at least seven Nazi-inspired murders in prisoner-of-war camps and

dozens of other incidents, 72 of which the Army termed suicides. Many of the suicides apparently resulted from Nazi intimidation—typically in the form of threats against the victim's family in Germany.

Most of the seven murder victims were men accused of treason by their fellow prisoners; the murderers maintained that they were merely doing their duty for the fatherland. In fact, several of the victims apparently had committed acts that could be construed as treasonous to Germany's Nazi regime. The charges included collaboration with the Americans and supplying military information.

A grisly example of Nazi retribution was enacted on the night of November 4, 1943, at Camp Tonkawa, Oklahoma. A kangaroo court consisting of 200 POWs convened in the mess hall. The accused was Corporal Johann Kunze, who was blamed for writing a note to U.S. officials containing information about the port of Hamburg useful to the Allies in planning bombing raids (in fact, the information was widely available in American magazines). The prisoners' leader announced there was a traitor in their midst, and read the note. Immediately a gang of prisoners began shouting Kunze's name; they beat him to death with clubs and broken milk bottles.

This action was dealt with in stern fashion by American authorities. Five veteran sergeants of the Afrika Korps were arrested and tried for murder by a U.S. Army court-martial. They were convicted and later hanged on a gallows rigged in an elevator shaft at Fort Leavenworth, Kansas. They were the first POWs to be executed in the United States.

The trial judge advocate, or prosecutor, in the Kunze case was a young Army lawyer named Leon Jaworski, who many years later would serve as U.S. special prosecutor in the Watergate investigations. In his autobiography, *Confession and Avoidance*, Jaworski recalled another murder case during the reign of violence. A young German at Camp Chaffee, Arkansas, was beaten to death, apparently because he had volunteered for paid work not required of him. Though six prisoners were suspected of taking part in the murder, Jaworski prosecuted only their leader, who did not physically participate in the crime but was convicted of it (and served a long prison term for it). Witnesses, fearful for their own lives, were reluctant to speak up; Jaworski had to transfer them to other camps where they could talk freely. To discourage claims of mistreatment, Jaworski, who spoke German, used an interpreter. "I never abused a suspect or raised a hand to one," Jaworski wrote, "although at times their arrogance made me want to slap them silly."

To avoid inflaming the American public, the Army conducted such trials in secret. But to adhere to the law and to ensure reciprocal treatment of American POWs, representatives of neutral Switzerland attended the court sessions and transmitted complete records to Germany. Altogether, 14 German prisoners were convicted of murder and hanged, though none was executed until after Germany's surrender on May 8, 1945. Until shortly before that, the United States was trying to exchange the condemned Germans for American POWs facing death in Germany on similar charges. Fortunately the advance of Allied Forces ensured the rescue of the Americans before their sentences were carried out.

The biggest mass trial of German POWs involved seven U-boat crewmen accused of beating and strangling fellow submariner Werner Drechsler. In this case there seemed to be little question that the victim had betrayed his countrymen. After his capture at sea as a rescued seaman from the sunken U-118, Drechsler cooperated with U.S. Navy interrogators and was sent to an interrogation center at Fort Meade, Maryland. Furnished with a cover as Petty Officer Leimi, he was confined for seven months in cells at Fort Meade with other U-boat sailors, where he talked with them about their submarines and presumably collected information for his interrogators.

On March 12, 1944, Drechsler was transferred to the POW camp at Papago Park, Arizona, which housed mostly German U-boat crewmen, including some members of the U-118 crew. This transfer occurred even though the Navy had warned the Army to keep Drechsler segregated from other Naval POWs. The other prisoners at Papago Park compared notes and quickly confirmed that Drechsler was Leimi and had spied on them. A few hours after his arrival at Papago Park, Drechsler was hanging from a rafter in a compound shower room. In August 1945, seven German submariners were hanged at Fort Leavenworth for his murder.

Werner Drechsler would probably have been no better protected had he done his spying for the British. Nazi discipline and terror were rampant in British and Canadian

Italian prisoners of war pause in their work on an English farm to enjoy tea served by the farmer's daughters. Guards (background) escorted large groups that worked on agricultural projects, but many prisoners were allowed to live unguarded on farms where they were employed.

camps too. Medicine Hat camp in Alberta, largely populated by Afrika Korps troops, was called a "battleground of political mayhem," and at a camp near Banff, hardened Nazi prisoners captured their Canadian camp commander and held him hostage in an attempt to extract special privileges. In several Canadian camps, POW leaders were reported to have ordered some men to commit suicide.

In the American camps, the worst of the violence subsided during the spring of 1944. No one knows precisely why, but waning German fortunes of war may have been a factor. In the summer, the camps began to receive the second great wave of German prisoners—taken during the Allied invasion of France in June. The influx nearly doubled the total U.S. POW population; it reached more than 400,000 during the next six months. Compared with the prisoners of the first wave, the new arrivals were less politically indoctrinated and more realistic; they had seen firsthand the beginnings of Germany's collapse, and they were therefore less responsive to Nazi pressure and Nazi appeals to their faith in Germany's future. U.S. authorities, in order to spread the word and discourage the Nazis, deliberately sprinkled these new prisoners among camps all over the country. Little by little the tension eased.

But as the violence subsided, its effects were touching off a wave of concern in the U.S. press. In newspaper editorials, columns and letters to the editor, writers suggested that the Army should not only isolate the Nazis responsible for the reign of terror, but it should also establish a program with a more ambitious aim: to educate German POWs in the theory and practice of democracy.

Early in the spring of 1944, two of the most vocal proponents of the reeducation idea were Dorothy Thompson, a widely read syndicated columnist, and Dorothy Bromley, women's page editor of the *New York Herald Tribune*. Both of them had the ear of the President's wife, Eleanor Roosevelt. Eleanor talked to Franklin, and the President sent word down the chain of command.

In fact, a plan had been lying on a shelf at the War Department for about a year. The plan had been drawn up in mid-1943 as a possible method of controlling Nazi domination in the camps and then shelved as "inadvisable" by the office of the Provost Marshal General. But now the plan had presidential approval, and the bureaucrats were in the happy position of merely having to dust it off. Secretary of War Henry Stimson, in outlining the program to Secretary of State Cordell Hull on April 9, 1944, declared that the objective of reeducation "should not be the improbable one of Americanizing the prisoners, but the feasible one of imbuing them with respect for the quality and potency of American institutions." In this aspect of POW policy, the United States was ahead of its Allies: A counterpart British reeducation plan did not get under way for more than a year.

From the beginning, the U.S. reeducation program was wrapped in the tightest secrecy. For one thing, the War Department feared that if German camp authorities heard about the program, they might try to indoctrinate American prisoners. Another consideration was that if the German POWs knew they were about to be reeducated they might resist—for instance, by refusing to attend indoctrination sessions. Perhaps the most important reason for secrecy was that the program seemed to be in clear violation of the Geneva Convention's prohibition against prisoner indoctrination. However, War Department planners found a loophole in the Convention's Article 17: "So far as possible, belligerents shall encourage intellectual diversions and sports organized by prisoners of war." Accordingly, the reeducation of German prisoners was publicly veiled under an innocuous name, "Intellectual Diversion Program." The fact that it included American sports gave it further respectability.

The program, which began in the fall of 1944, was run by the specially created POW Special Projects Division of the U.S. Army Provost Marshal General's office. The division assembled an impressive team of American scholars—both military and civilian—under Lieut. Colonel Edward Davison, a poet and teacher. This team was a kind of board of directors to supervise the materials of the program: Through books, movies, newspapers and the classroom, said a division memo, "the prisoners would be given facts, objectively presented but so selected and assembled as to correct misinformation and prejudices surviving Nazi conditioning." The POWs were also to be required to study English.

Most of the publications and classroom curricula were churned out by a carefully selected group of some 85 German prisoners—all volunteers—who were linguists, writers and former professors with reputations as dedicated anti-

In June 1945, German prisoners of war view films of concentration-camp atrocities; both American and British officials required POWs to attend such screenings. Most could not believe that the films were authentic; one anti-Nazi prisoner later wrote, "I needed ten, twenty, thirty years before I could grasp the abomination of the Nazi regime."

Nazis. They worked at the division's "Idea Factory," which was located first at an isolated camp in upstate New York and then at Fort Philip Kearney on an island in Rhode Island's Narragansett Bay. To preserve secrecy and to protect the prisoners from possible future reprisals by other German POWs, the Factory received its mail through Camp Niagara, New York, an ordinary POW camp.

Out on the island, the Factory was probably the most relaxed camp in the world. There were no guards, no watchtowers. The prisoners traveled on the ferry to the mainland in comparative freedom, socializing en route with American civilians who had no idea they were talking to German POWs. The prisoners were all officers, but in order to practice the democratic ideas they were preaching, they renounced their German ranks.

In this atmosphere of freedom, the prisoners labored with enthusiasm; morale and creativity were high. They reviewed the books coming into the camp libraries, most of which were sent from Germany through the International Red Cross and International YMCA, and weeded out the volumes containing Nazi propaganda. They commissioned a special series of 24 German-language paperback books that were sold in camp canteens for 25 cents each—reprinting classics by such German authors as Thomas Mann, and introducing American writers such as Ernest Hemingway and William Saroyan. The prisoners prepared and translated books and pamphlets about American geography, history and government for use in the camp classrooms.

Sheet music was circulated that emphasized American themes and featured such composers as John Philip Sousa and George Gershwin. To comply with the Geneva Convention's article on mental diversion, and to improve morale, the Factory oversaw the distribution of equipment for sports, including such popular American pastimes as baseball, basketball and horseshoes. American sports must have found some willing converts: After the War, basketball was

a common diversion on ships that carried former POWs back to Europe.

The Factory's most impressive product was a handsome biweekly newspaper, *Der Ruf (The Call)*. Under the editorship of POWs Gustav René Hocke, a prize-winning novelist, and Curt Vinz, a former German newspaper publisher, *Der Ruf* was lively and diversified: It included news from the battlefronts, reviews of performances by New York's Metropolitan Opera and discussions of American social issues—even articles on such ticklish subjects as racism.

Some Nazi prisoners took violent exception to *Der Ruf;* when the first issue went on sale for five cents in camp canteens on March 6, 1945, they set stacks of the newspapers on fire. Only 11,000 copies of this first issue were circulated, but seven months later circulation stood at 73,000. An unexpected dividend of publishing *Der Ruf* was its apparently benign influence on camp newspapers published by prisoners; monitors at the Factory saw the number of such newspapers adjudged pro-Nazi dwindle in a matter of months from 33 to only one.

Along with *Der Ruf,* materials for the reeducation program went out from the Factory to the camps, where the difficult task of coordination at each base fell to a specially assigned U.S. officer, the assistant executive officer (AEO). Assigned to a camp after only a week's training at Fort Slocum, New York, the AEO had to find inconspicuous ways to identify and segregate Nazis, and shift the leadership to prisoners who were open to reeducation. Sometimes the American camp commander was the biggest obstacle to the AEO's effort. Several of the AEOs were Jewish, and in at least one camp the Jewish AEO had to be replaced because an anti-Semitic commanding officer encouraged prisoners and American enlisted personnel to ignore him.

Explaining American racism in the treatment of blacks was a continuing challenge for the reeducation program, which confronted the fact that Axis POWs were sometimes treated better than American blacks: *The New York Times* reported one incident in Salina, Kansas, where German prisoners were served at a whites-only lunch counter while a black GI stood and watched in frustration. At Fort Lawton,

Washington, a group of more than 50 black soldiers became so angry at the whites' treatment of Italian cobelligerents that the blacks staged a midnight raid on the Italians' barracks, sending 26 men to the hospital; the body of another was found swinging from a nearby tree.

At many of the camps, the AEO arranged for universities in the area to conduct extension courses for the prisoners by sending in professors to lecture on civics, American history and geography. The AEO at Camp Mackall, North Carolina, managed to stage an election for camp spokesman in which the prisoners grouped themselves into four political parties. At Camp Butner in the same state, the AEO taught a lesson in tolerance by arranging for a local Jewish merchant to supply hard-to-get musical instruments.

The contest for the POWs' minds focused on the nightly camp movie. Before the reeducation program was introduced, movies had often been selected by the POW camp spokesman with the aim of exposing the shortcomings of American democracy. Among the favorites had been movies such as *Lady Scarface* (about a lady gangster), *Seven Miles from Alcatraz* (about Nazi spies) and *Legion of the Lawless* (about a crooked citizens' committee).

Now, however, the AEOs tried to present a more positive image; they promoted showings of 115 feature films approved by the Factory. This list eliminated gangster and violent cowboy movies, and almost anything that showed slums or the darker side of American life. The emphasis, said a Factory memo, was on movies that "reflected the American scene without distortion and which fostered respect for our democratic institutions." This meant that prisoners saw "wholesome" movies such as *Abe Lincoln in Illinois* and *The Adventures of Tom Sawyer,* as well as a number of government-produced documentaries about life in the United States. Revenue from the box office (prisoners had to pay 15 cents admission), along with money from the sales of books and *Der Ruf,* helped to finance the reeducation program.

The veil of secrecy surrounding reeducation was lifted after Germany's surrender. At the same time, as part of the program, the prisoners were shown several hitherto restricted government documentaries showing scenes of German concentration and death camps. The audience reaction was decidedly mixed. At Camp Butner, 1,000 prisoners were so moved by the films that they burned their German uniforms. At Eglin Field, Florida, POWs took up a collection and contributed $2,371 to U.S. war charities. But many POWs refused to accept the filmed evidence; a survey of 20,000 prisoners indicated that only 36 per cent believed that Germany had committed these atrocities.

The long-range effects of the Intellectual Diversion Program were difficult to measure, but the immediate results were encouraging. During the spring of 1945, German prisoners at a previously pro-Nazi camp in Florence, Arizona, offered condolences to the U.S. Army upon the death of President Roosevelt. POWs at other camps called upon Germany to surrender. Some POWs even volunteered to fight in the war against Japan—an idea that was seriously considered by U.S. military authorities.

But much of the value of the program was undermined in its final months by a succession of events that seemed inconsistent with the ideals of universal justice and democracy that had been so fervently espoused. The War was over, and much of the original motivation for America's kid-gloved treatment of POWs had disappeared; the War Department no longer had to worry about U.S. prisoners in German hands. Now, U.S. authorities curtailed some canteen privileges and severely cut back the quality of the camp diet—serving margarine instead of butter, fewer eggs, and beef only twice a month instead of several times a week. Officially, the cutbacks in food were attributed to domestic shortages, but many POWs saw them as a form of reprisal for the newly revealed atrocities in the concentration camps and for deteriorating treatment suffered by some American prisoners during Germany's disintegration in the last months of the War.

What probably did the most damage to the prisoners' new view of America was the delay—stemming from their importance to the U.S. economy—in getting home. It was more than a year after the end of the War before the last German prisoner left American soil (though many were not in a hurry to return because conditions at home were so bad and some wanted to stay permanently in the United States).

Many were sent to work in war-ravaged European countries—chiefly France and Belgium. But for 123,000 German POWs the real disillusionment came when they were sent to work camps in Britain, where they spent two more years and went through another "reeducation."

The British reeducation program, which had started after the German surrender in 1945, was much more ambitious than the American program. While the Americans emphasized the political structure of democracy, the British tried to provide their POWs with a new social awareness to replace the Nazi insensitivity that had been a way of life for many Germans. According to Henry Faulk, the British official who developed the program, the British reeducation effort "was directed at change in the group as an organism" rather than being designed to change the ideas of individuals.

Like the Americans, the British used books, lectures, films and newspapers in order to stimulate a discussion among the prisoners that they hoped would lead to a spontaneous anti-Nazi consensus. Although English was taught to prisoners who wanted to learn it, the British did not require it as the Americans had. Like the Americans, the British had difficulty evaluating the success of their program, although they did note that younger prisoners were more receptive to reeducation than older men were. When they rescreened groups of prisoners after many months of reeducation, the British were gratified to find a definite shift from "blacks" to "grays." Nevertheless, the program did not produce large numbers of new "whites."

It was even harder for the British to decide whether the reeducation programs had any lasting effect on postwar Germany; after all, Germans at home were rejecting the Nazi political system at the same time because Hitler had failed. Furthermore, it was impossible to measure the effect on public attitudes of the group of so-called white prisoners repatriated early from Britain in the hope that they would help build a new Germany: As an identifiable social force, said Faulk, they "vanished without a trace."

As the War began to wind down, the joyful prospect of peace was clouded for many prisoners by the fear that the cease-fire might bring them death instead of liberation. Because World War II was so cruel a conflict, it evoked thoughts of primitive times when war had no rules, and captors held—and exercised—a fatal power over captives. Allied prisoners in German and Japanese hands had a sense—more or less justified by what they could see and hear—that Nazi fanaticism or Oriental pride might, in the face of defeat, lead to mass slaughter of POWs. The months, weeks and days before the final cease-fire thus became a time of painful suspense. Relief from the worst of the pressure came to most prisoners with the approach of victory in Europe; the process was more harrowing in the Pacific.

For many, however, the anxiety did not necessarily end with the victory or defeat of their homeland. Condemned by Stalin, liberated Soviet prisoners exchanged the misery of German captivity for the oblivion of death or penal servitude in the U.S.S.R. On the losing side, some Axis prisoners had to endure months and even years of confinement and labor after the end of hostilities.

The last months before liberation were the worst of their captivity for most of the 260,000 British and American prisoners of Hitler's crumbling Third Reich. As the Red Army converged from the east and the British and U.S. forces from the west, prisoners were marched from one camp to another to keep them inside Germany's diminishing domain. Allied planes bombarding the roads and railways made the delivery of vital Red Cross food parcels difficult and sometimes killed or injured prisoners on the march.

Tension began to build early in 1945. At Stalag Luft 3, the vast German camp for 10,300 British and American airmen near Sagan, the news crackled from the prisoners' clandestine radio on January 12 and quickly spread through the camp's six compounds: The long-awaited offensive by the Soviet Army massed along the German-Polish border had begun; advance elements of the Red Army were reported only 165 miles east of Sagan. Now, at long last, liberation seemed imminent.

During the next two weeks, as the Red Army drew nearer, the excitement grew at Sagan but so did the doubts and fears. Everyone, including the guards, offered a rumor: The

6

A fear of mass slaughter
"One step nearer home, and going to take another"
Risky plans for rescue
Vitamins and a soft diet at Camp Lucky Strike
The tragic drama of forced repatriation
"A tableau from the Russia of 1812"
Grim portents for the prisoners of Japan
Forty gallons of fruit salad
Living "like Oriental despots"

THE ANXIOUS DELIVERANCE

prisoners would be evacuated to the West; they would be held as hostages to prevent the Russians from taking Sagan; they would all be shot.

By January 26, with the Red Army a little more than 20 miles east of Sagan, the apocalyptic rumors were so rampant that the camp's highest-ranking prisoner, Brigadier General Arthur Vanaman, called a meeting. The men, anxious to hear him, gathered in the center compound. Although Vanaman let deputies run the compounds and generally kept a low profile, the Sagan prisoners attributed their comparative well-being to his efforts. Sagan was one of the best camps in Germany; discipline there was good, and the camp was well supplied with Red Cross food parcels.

Vanaman strode into the auditorium wearing his full-dress Army Air Forces uniform and carrying a Bible under his right arm. He began by chewing out the men for spreading rumors and destroying morale. He went on to urge them to "stand together as one team, ready to face whatever may come." Finally, the general ordered the men to return to their barracks and spend an hour in prayer.

Vanaman was a religious man, but he was also practical. He had already instructed his compound commanders to get ready for possible evacuation; the prisoners were sewing gloves cut from discarded overcoats and building sleds from bedboards. Vanaman had also issued orders on how to deal with the most feared eventuality: At the first sign of any attempt by the Germans to kill prisoners, the men of Sagan were to set in motion detailed plans for a desperate mass breakout, storming the guard stations with knives, clubs and other crude weapons.

The following night, January 27, 1945, the prisoners learned that their immediate fate was to be neither liberation nor liquidation. The German guards gave them an hour's notice to pack and prepare to march west. About 11 p.m., under falling snow, the prisoners began filing out of their compounds in columns of five, with food parcels slung over their backs in blanket rolls and piled high on their improvised sleds. Emptying the camp took all night; the Germans drove the leading columns hard all the next day, and the prisoners had covered nearly 30 miles before they were allowed to rest. By that time, the line of march straggled west for some 20 miles.

In their great haste to evacuate Sagan, the German administrators had made few provisions for food and billets. After two days of marching in the snow and cold, and sleeping at night in unheated barns and churches, prisoners and guards alike began to fail. Hundreds of men suffered from frostbite and scores developed pneumonia. Some men died. A Texan named Kenneth Simmons fought off fever and chills—and periods during which he spat blood. Like thousands of others, he had one bright thought to keep him going. "I must have said it a thousand times," Simmons wrote later. "I am one step nearer home, and I am going to take another."

Though they knew the procession was heading in the right direction—westward—none of the prisoners knew the destination of this journey. Finally, after a weary week, the last groups of marchers stumbled into Spremberg, a rail junction about 55 miles west of Sagan. Here, General Vanaman and one of his American compound commanders, Colonel Delmar Spivey, left the other prisoners. According to rumor, they were being taken to Berlin to strike some sort of deal with the Nazis for the prisoners' release. Everyone else was loaded onto cattle cars and shipped farther west. They ended up at four separate POW camps where they crowded in among the previous occupants and once more began sweating out their approaching liberation.

The very nearness of freedom was a torment. Rumors persisted that the prisoners might survive present hardships only long enough to be held hostage or struck down by their captors in a last-ditch defense of the German homeland. That these rumors were not the mere fantasies of "wire-happy" prisoners is demonstrated by the experience of Vanaman and Spivey. After being separated from their men at Spremberg, they were transferred to a large prison camp at Luckenwalde, south of Berlin.

Late in March, Vanaman and Spivey were summoned to Berlin to meet SS General Gottlob Berger, Germany's chief administrator of POWs (page 175). Berger told them that, several months previously, Hitler had ordered him to collect all British and U.S. air officers from German camps and enclose them in downtown target areas of Berlin and other major cities. Hitler believed that using prisoners as hostages would force the Allies to suspend bombing attacks.

Like many of the Führer's orders in those final months of

the War, this one was never put into effect. Following their meeting with Berger, both American officers gained their freedom. Berger, a member of one of several groups of German leaders seeking a negotiated surrender independently of Hitler, asked Vanaman and Spivey to plead their cause with the Allies. Then he had the Americans escorted south to neutral Switzerland.

Beyond Hitler's order to Berger was an even more direct threat to the lives of Allied airmen held in Germany. In February 1945, not long after the march west by the prisoners from Sagan, Hitler's Minister of Propaganda, Joseph Goebbels, proposed a drastic measure to the Führer: Take all of the Allied airmen from their prison camps and shoot them. He reasoned that liquidation of the airmen would bring the Allied bombing to a halt and dissuade the Germans from surrendering on the Western Front, for fear of being killed in reprisal.

Word of Goebbels' proposal may have leaked out, for soon Allied planners met in France to consider the possibility of arming the POWs in Germany. By coded mail, requests for arms from British prisoners were pouring into MI-9. In fact, prisoners in some camps had already begun to arm themselves, bartering coffee, cigarettes and chocolate with their increasingly demoralized guards in exchange for pistols and even submachine guns.

The Allied planners discussed two possibilities: mailing small arms in disguised relief parcels, and supplying the camps by parachute. Both alternatives, the planners finally concluded, were too risky. Discovery by the Germans might provide them with the excuse to start shooting prisoners.

The meeting adjourned after the planners had agreed on one important safety measure. Allied parachute teams would be ordered to stand by; if a massacre was threatened at any of the camps, the teams would be dropped in.

Photographed by the Soviets in 1945 after they were shot—possibly by German captors to forestall liberation—these Russians included at least one (right

The Allied planners at the February meeting apparently did not consider a second possible means of rescuing prisoners: quick thrusts on the ground through enemy lines.

Lieut. General George S. Patton, however, did recognize the opportunity. Patton and his Third Army had crossed the Rhine, raced 45 miles to the German town of Aschaffenburg and seized a bridgehead on the Main River. From that advance position, Patton saw a beautiful objective for a raid: Hammelburg, where a camp held several thousand prisoners of a dozen different nationalities. How many Americans were there no one knew, but Patton expected to find 300 to 400. The camp was behind German lines, about 60 miles to the northeast of Aschaffenburg. Patton's plan was to send a special task force to Hammelburg, liberate the Americans and bring them back to the U.S. lines at the Main.

Patton revealed only to his closest aides a highly personal reason for the raid on Hammelburg. A few weeks before, he had learned that his son-in-law, Lieut. Colonel John K. Waters, captured in North Africa in February 1943 and imprisoned in Poland, was now at Hammelburg, having been marched west in January to avoid the Red Army.

Patton wanted to commit to this special mission an entire combat command, a mixed contingent of more than 3,500 men with considerable armor. But he was dissuaded by a Third Army corps commander in charge of the main assault northward, who did not want to spare so large a force. The compromise was a task force less than one tenth the size of a combat command; it comprised 294 officers and men and 53 vehicles, including 15 tanks, three self-propelled 105mm assault guns and 27 half-track personnel carriers.

Command of the task force was entrusted to Captain Abraham Baum. In his eight months of combat in France and Belgium, Abe Baum had commanded other special task forces with such distinction that he had acquired a respect-

foreground) in the kind of striped suit issued to concentration-camp inmates. The corpses were found, according to the Soviet picture caption, at Zonenburg Jail.

173

ful nickname: "Able." But this was his toughest assignment, a 120-mile round trip through enemy territory with no hope of reinforcement if he ran into trouble.

Shortly before midnight on March 26, he maneuvered his Task Force Baum into takeoff position just beyond the bridgehead at Aschaffenburg. Only then did Baum learn that one of the purposes of his mission—perhaps the main purpose—was to rescue Patton's son-in-law.

For a while after the column started rolling, Baum's mission went beautifully. Task Force Baum thundered through several blacked-out towns, taking only small-arms fire from Germans who were too surprised to fight back in strength. But as Baum raced along the dark roads, he passed through territory occupied by units of the German Seventh Army; these sounded the alert, and shortly before dawn the task force began to encounter trouble. At Lohr, about halfway to Hammelburg, the lead tank was put out of action by a *Panzerfaust*—the German antitank grenade launcher. Farther along, at Gmünden, two more tanks were lost when German defenders blew up a bridge and forced Baum to detour to the north.

Shortly after noon on March 27, twelve hours into his mission, Baum approached the town of Hammelburg. He turned south to begin searching for the prison camp and ran into a column of eight German *Panzerjäger*—tank destroyers. The resulting two-hour battle cost Baum valuable time, as well as three tanks, five half-tracks and two jeeps, including the vehicles carrying spare gas for the return trip.

Baum soon spotted the camp, but a company of German combat engineers sent to defend the camp were entrenched outside the fence. His task force had to fight its way to the barbed-wire enclosure, unavoidably firing into the compound as they engaged the Germans. In the confusion, the German camp commandant surrendered, turning control of the camp over to the American POWs—but leaving the engineer defenders still blazing away at Baum's men.

The stage was now set for irony—and near-tragedy. To stop the shooting, four American prisoners volunteered to serve in a truce party. In the company of a German officer, they walked out through the camp gate carrying a white sheet rigged on a pole and a homemade American flag on an improvised flagstaff. The American officer in the lead was a 39-year-old West Pointer and an avid sportsman. He was Patton's son-in-law, Johnny Waters.

Suddenly, as the little group headed toward the liberators of Task Force Baum, a German soldier with a rifle appeared from behind a building just outside the compound. Waters, trying to tell the man not to shoot, shouted at him. The German fired. The bullet struck Waters just below the right hip, smashing the bone. He lay on the ground, numb from the waist down, thinking, "You son of a bitch, you've ruined my fishing." The others carried Waters back through the camp gate into the prison hospital.

Minutes later, the combat engineers retreated. Three of the prisoners retrieved the truce party's makeshift Stars and Stripes and ran it up the camp flagpole. Then, while the POWs cheered like fans at a football game, a tank from Task Force Baum smashed through the barbed wire. A prisoner leaped onto the tank and, with magnificent nonchalance, asked one of the crewmen, "Got a cigarette, buddy?"

Following the tank, Abe Baum's jeep pulled into the compound and was engulfed by exuberant prisoners. But Baum's own elation soon turned to frustration and despair. He was shocked to find that the camp contained 1,230 Americans, far more than the 300 or so he had expected. The prisoners, in turn, were bitterly disappointed to learn that their liberators were a mere task force and not the front ranks of Patton's mighty army. Only about 200 prisoners could ride aboard the half-tracks and tanks. Hundreds of others formed up to march alongside. But many of the prisoners were ill and underweight, obviously in no shape to trek 60 miles through enemy territory. They stayed behind, along with the seriously wounded Johnny Waters.

Well after dark on that night of March 27, the task force prepared to move out with its retinue of liberated prisoners. Baum sent ahead a reconnaissance unit to the southwest to find a way around the German defenses. The search encountered German road blocks, and the unit lost three tanks to tank and *Panzerfaust* fire. Baum decided to regroup on a nearby hill and wait until morning to attempt a breakthrough. During the night, all but about a dozen of the prisoners accompanying him decided to return to the camp. One POW remembers that as they reentered the compound—through the same hole made earlier in the wire by one of Baum's tanks—a sympathetic German guard said, in

SS GENERAL GOTTLOB BERGER

RED CROSS LIFE LINE FOR HUNGRY PRISONERS

As the Reich began to break up in the winter and spring of 1945—with Red Army troops hammering on the gates of Berlin and Allied planes dropping bombs on Germany around the clock—food and medicines for Allied prisoners became scarce. The shortages were especially acute because the Germans were marching many POWs from the Eastern Front to central and southern Germany to keep them out of Russian hands. Soon the available prisons overflowed with cold, hungry men.

In order to save lives, the International Red Cross—in cooperation with the Allies and Germany—made plans to send emergency aid from Geneva. With the permission of the Reich's POW administrator, General Gottlob Berger, the Red Cross assembled a fleet of trucks (many supplied by the United States) to supplement the deteriorating German railway service. The marked trucks traveled on assigned routes known to Allied bomber crews; only once was a convoy mistakenly strafed.

By mid-June the trucks had traveled one million miles to deliver 6,600 tons of food and medical supplies, and win a race with chaos and starvation.

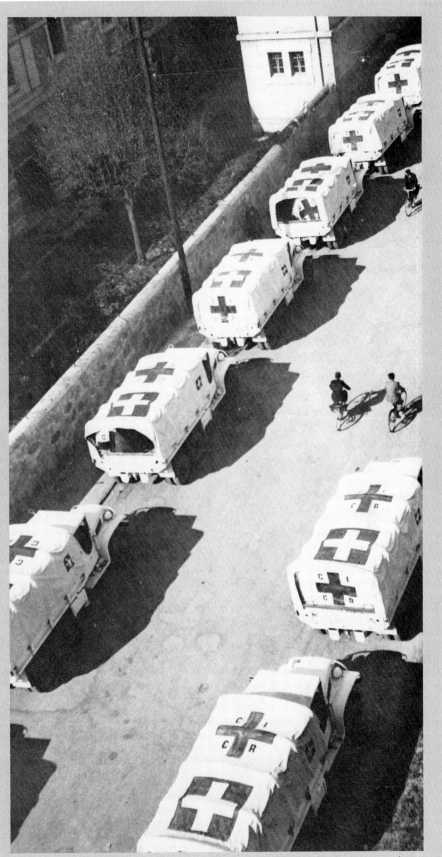

Red Cross markings identify trucks carrying food parcels to Allied prisoners of war.

English, "Get some sleep, boys. You had a hard night."

During the night, a substantial force of Germans—five tanks, five tank destroyers and two companies of infantry heavily armed with *Panzerfäuste*—moved in around Baum's force, now reduced to 240 able-bodied men who had not slept for two nights. As Baum loaded up and started moving out, the Germans opened fire. One after another, Baum's vehicles went up in flames. Baum ordered his men to abandon them and try to get back to safety on foot.

Only a handful of Baum's original force of 294 managed to work their way to the Allied lines. The mission cost the lives of 25 soldiers. The rest, including Baum, who was tracked down just before dark that evening of March 28, were taken prisoner, joining behind barbed wire the other American POWs who had tasted a few hours of freedom. The next day, Baum, who had been wounded three times during the mission, marked his 24th birthday in the prison hospital at Hammelburg as a fellow patient of Johnny Waters, the man he had come to liberate.

On April 6, 1945, scarcely a week after Baum's ill-starred raid, the camp at Hammelburg fell, without a shot being fired, to Lieut. General Alexander Patch's U.S. Seventh Army. But the fates of Waters and Baum were still intertwined. At Patton's request, the Seventh Army brought in a plane to evacuate his wounded son-in-law to an Allied hospital. (A highly capable leader, Waters would become a four-star general after the War.)

However, Waters' would-be rescuer, Abe Baum, was not on the plane with him. Indeed, in the fuss over Johnny Waters, several score other wounded and sick, including Baum, were overlooked and did not receive for another three days the medical attention that Waters got.

As April ended, liberation of prisoners in western Germany by rapidly advancing U.S. and British forces proceeded more smoothly. Fears for the safety of the POWs—and thoughts of special air or ground rescue missions—largely subsided. In the face of overwhelming Allied superiority, the Germans at camp after camp simply gave up, often without a fight, and the prisoners were safe and free at last.

On May 8, Germany officially capitulated, and the status of liberated Allied prisoners changed forever. Now being moved by the thousands into special reception camps in France and Belgium, they were no longer *Kriegsgefangenen*—the German word for prisoners of war. They were now known officially as RAMPs (Repatriated Allied Military Personnel). With their new category came the inevitable "processing"—delousing, medical examinations, endless forms to fill out, and doctors' exhortations (seldom heeded) to stick to a soft diet until their shrunken stomachs could adjust to three square meals a day.

Liberated British and Commonwealth POWs were assembled in centers in France and Belgium and then sent to England fairly rapidly. American RAMPs were collected in a large staging area called Camp Lucky Strike, where they had to wait to be shipped home. Lucky Strike was a vast tent city near the French port of Le Havre, and at one time in May bulged with some 48,000 former prisoners.

The average Allied prisoner had lost 35 to 45 pounds—mostly in the final months of captivity when bombing of roads and railroads kept Red Cross parcels from getting through—and a large percentage suffered from dysentery and other diet-related disorders. When a troupe of USO entertainers arrived at Lucky Strike, hardly anyone watched their show. "Don't you want to see these beautiful girls?" a Red Cross worker asked. "Well, ma'am," said one former prisoner, "they are feeding me 12 vitamin pills a day now, but before I'll be interested in women again they'll have to feed me 24."

Though the men at Lucky Strike grumbled about the delays in getting a ship home to the United States—some RAMPs had to wait for up to six weeks—they fared far better than their compatriots who had been liberated by the Russians. Problems had begun during the previous winter when the Red Army overran German camps containing Allied prisoners in Poland and East Prussia. While the Germans had evacuated many of the prisoners before the Russians arrived, some were left behind and others had escaped during the enforced trek west. Before long, several thousand British and American liberated prisoners were roaming around Poland or being held in Red Army collection centers. The Russians paid little attention to the men and left them with insufficient food and medical care.

The return of these men to their own people—and the repatriation of thousands of others—had been built into the agreements about postwar arrangements that had been reached in February of 1945 by Premier Stalin, President Roosevelt and Prime Minister Churchill at Yalta in the Crimea. The accord dealing with prisoners of war provided for the prompt transfer of the captured from areas where they had been set free into the hands of authorities from their home countries. In practice, the agreement contained a number of grave defects that caused many of the prisoners a great deal of harm.

Erratic compliance with the agreement posed additional problems. American repatriation teams were supposed to have the right of "immediate access" to U.S. prisoners liberated by the Red Army. But Stalin refused repeated requests by American officials in Moscow, even by President Roosevelt, to allow planes to land in Poland to evacuate the prisoners. The Premier assured Roosevelt that the liberated prisoners were being transported eastward some 600 miles from the middle of Poland to Odessa, the Soviet port on the Black Sea. From there they could be taken home by ship.

Ambassador Harriman had reason for doubting Stalin when three American escapees turned up in Moscow in March after hitchhiking across Poland and western Russia. They reported that hundreds of Americans "were wandering in the rear of the Red Army searching for an American in authority and being ignored by the Russians."

Finally, Soviet officials did bring together at Odessa some 7,000 British and American prisoners who were evacuated in May on Allied ships that had carried home repatriated Soviet prisoners liberated in Western Europe. But during that spring of 1945, further problems developed as the Red Army liberated camps of Allied POWs in eastern Germany. When Soviet troops overran the camp at Fürstenberg, for example, they opened fire on American prisoners, killing about 50 and wounding several hundred; the Russians said they had mistaken the Americans for Hungarian soldiers who had fought as allies of Germany.

Prisoners in German camps relieved by the Red Army often had to endure delays of a month or more under Soviet guard before they were turned over to Allied forces. For example, the Red Army arrived at Luckenwalde on April 23 when the U.S. Ninth Army was just west of the Elbe River, less than 50 miles away. Because of red tape and Soviet truculence—on one occasion Russian soldiers actually fired shots above a convoy of U.S. trucks sent to fetch the prisoners—it was May 20 before all of the Allied prisoners were evacuated to safety behind the U.S. lines.

At Luckenwalde was Tommy Calnan, one of the most escape-minded members of the RAF; rather than wait for evacuation, he decided to take matters into his own hands. For Calnan, Russian liberation, with its armed sentries and lack of food, was too much like German captivity. Before the Red Army's arrival at Luckenwalde, Calnan and an Australian friend had found a pair of bicycles and hidden them in the camp; within a week of the Red Army's arrival they swapped Calnan's Rolex watch with a Soviet captain for a pair of passes to get them out the prison gate. Then, with small red flags affixed to their bicycles, they began pedaling furiously toward the Elbe and freedom.

Whenever they approached Russian soldiers, Calnan and his mate threw them the clenched-fist salute and boomed "*Zdrasti, tovarich!*" ("Greetings, comrade!"). A day later, they reached the American lines on the Elbe. To avoid the red tape of reception camps, they then hitched a succession of plane rides to Croydon, England, only to have a fussy immigration official detain them in a locked room. Calnan, an expert picklock after more than three years in captivity, started to jimmy the lock on the wooden door, but then changed his mind as he realized that—though still confined—he was technically free. If he escaped from his own government's agents, he would be an outlaw. In frustration, Calnan kicked the door so hard he split the lower panel; but he stayed put until the official released him.

For all of its procrastination in returning liberated American and British prisoners, the Soviet Union was quite eager to get back those of its own citizens who had been freed by the Western Allies. This impatience was doubly ironic in view of the fact that, for most of the War, Stalin had failed even to acknowledge the existence of the 5.7 million Soviet citizens taken prisoner by Germany. By the final months of the War in Europe, only about two million were still alive. There were also in Germany and Western Europe some two million Soviet civilian slave laborers, and several hundred thousand other Soviet citizens who had fled the U.S.S.R. since 1943, when the German Army was forced to retreat.

Now Stalin wanted them all back, not least the nearly one million Soviet personnel—including POWs and slave laborers—who had served in German uniform. These he presumably wanted to single out and punish as traitors.

The turncoats were not the only ones slated for punishment. Roughly half of all the Soviet prisoners in Europe were liberated and repatriated by the Red Army itself in Eastern Europe. Under the Yalta agreement, those in the hands of the Western Allies were to be promptly shipped home as well. In this instance, compliance was not the problem. Churchill and Roosevelt had had a cogent reason for yielding to the insistent Stalin on the repatriation agreement: They wanted to ensure the safety of their own nationals liberated by the Red Army. In thinking about the overall situation, no one on the Allied side imagined that Stalin was determined to treat all of his own captured countrymen—not just those who had worn German uniforms—as traitors upon their repatriation.

However expedient, Allied compliance with the Yalta agreement—as influenced by Soviet interpretation of the accord—ignored the interests of the prisoners themselves. Apparently no one in authority in the West thought of asking Russian prisoners what they felt might be in store for them after repatriation. Yet the tenor of their expectations was evident as early as September of 1944—six months before the Yalta Conference—when a general from the Red Army visited a prison camp in England that held about 3,000 Russians, including some whom the Allies had captured in German uniform in France. In *The Secret Betrayal*, Nikolai Tolstoy has described the talk between the general and the prisoners:

" 'What are you going to do with us when we return to Russia?' asked one of the prisoners.

" 'You don't need to worry about that,' replied the general. 'There is enough room in the Soviet fatherland for everyone.'

" 'The dog knows what happens to him when he steals bacon,' suggested another prisoner.

" 'You need not worry,' said the general, 'because you were forced to serve against us.'

" 'We were not forced,' someone said.

" 'Well, don't worry,' replied the general. 'The Soviets never treat people in bulk—we shall find out who amongst you are guilty and who not.'

"Then the general fingered a German uniform on one of the prisoners: 'And this we shall burn in a crematorium.'

" 'We know,' said a prisoner, 'and us inside them too!' "

Only two months after this conversation, as Britain began repatriating the first of some 32,000 Russians captured while in German service, the fears voiced by the prisoners proved to be justified. The Soviet prisoners were taken by ship to Odessa, and in several instances British sailors and others who had accompanied them returned with ominous news. The repatriates had hardly debarked, these witnesses reported, when firing squads began carrying out executions.

During the four-year period between 1943 and 1947, the Western Allies turned 2,272,000 Soviet citizens over to the U.S.S.R. How many of them went willingly will never be known; Nikolai Tolstoy suggests the proportion of volunteers for repatriation may have been about two thirds—many of them lured by the Soviets' promises, subsequently broken, to forgive those who had fallen into enemy hands.

Had any prisoners known about the secret Yalta agreement, they would have been justified in thinking they had a right to refuse repatriation; the agreement made no specific provision for forced return of Soviet citizens. Yet U.S. and British policy makers tended to interpret it as if it did, and unwillingness was opposed with force.

The tragic drama of forced repatriation even reached to the shores of America—and, for a time, led to reconsideration of the policy. By the end of the War in Europe, about 4,300 Russians captured in German uniform and imprisoned in the United States had been repatriated. But 154 Russians held at Fort Dix, New Jersey, had adamantly refused to go. On the morning of June 29, 1945, these men were told that they would be loaded on a ship that afternoon and returned to the Soviet Union. The men thereupon barricaded themselves in their barracks. To flush them out, American guards fired in tear-gas grenades; the men emerged brandishing mess-kit knives, table legs and other improvised weapons. The skirmish lasted for 30 minutes, leaving three U.S. soldiers and seven prisoners wounded.

Inside the barracks, the Americans found three prisoners hanging from the rafters, and 15 empty nooses—their use forestalled by the tear-gas attack. Widespread publicity about the incident forced the U.S. State Department to hesitate briefly, but two months later the group from Fort Dix was shipped to Germany and turned over to the U.S.S.R.

Perhaps the cruelest aspect of forced repatriation was the Allied failure to screen Russians who were not Soviet citizens. The United States and Britain defined as a Soviet citizen anyone born or resident in the prewar boundaries of the U.S.S.R. who had not acquired another nationality. By this definition, the old émigrés who had left the Soviet Union 20 years earlier—after the Communist Revolution and civil war of 1918-1920—should have been excluded. Such was the haste of the Allies to court Soviet good will, however, that many old czarists were caught in the net of repatriation.

The most outrageous incident took place in southern Austria during the massive British roundup of German-armed Cossacks in the weeks following the end of the War in Europe. One such group handed over to the Red Army consisted of some 20,000 men of the XV Cossack Cavalry Corps, which under German General Hellmuth von Pannwitz had made its way north from Yugoslavia, after battling the Partisans of Marshal Tito for a year and a half, and had surrendered to the British on May 10, 1945. Except for their German officers, these Cossacks were nearly all Soviet citizens—former POWs or anti-Stalin volunteers recruited during the German occupation of their homeland—and thus candidates for repatriation under the Yalta agreement.

But another large group of Cossacks who surrendered to the British in southern Austria was quite different. This group, numbering about 24,000 men, women and children, had been living at Tolmezzo in northern Italy since September 1944 when the Germans occupying the area gave them sanctuary there. Though the majority were Soviet citizens who had fled the U.S.S.R. during the German retreat, many others were prewar émigrés who, hoping for a rebirth of the old Cossack nation, had joined their brethren in Italy.

Few of the Cossacks at Tolmezzo had actually fought in an organized fashion under the German banner; military activities in Italy had generally been limited to skirmishes

A prisoner-of-war barracks near Munich stands deserted following evacuation of the last Allied prisoners in May 1945. When the Third Army reached the camp on April 29, it contained 100,000 prisoners— 60,000 POWs had been shuttled from Eastern Europe as the perimeters of the Reich shrank. After the Allies promised that liberated prisoners would not fight again in Europe, the Germans stopped moving them.

against the Italian partisans. As the War wound down, the Cossacks came under increasing pressure from partisans. They left Tolmezzo on April 28, 1945, just 10 days before the end of the War in Europe, and began an arduous march north toward Austria, where the Cossacks hoped to surrender to the Allies. Fending off partisan attacks, they made their way through the snow-covered Alps.

The long Cossack procession presented an extraordinary spectacle. A British officer who saw them later in Austria wrote: "Their basic uniform was German, but with their fur Cossack caps, their mournful Dundreary whiskers, their knee-high riding boots, and their roughly made, horse-drawn carts bearing all their worldly goods and chattels, including wife and family, there could be no mistaking them for anything but Russians. They were a tableau from the Russia of 1812."

By the second week in May, the Cossacks had surrendered to the British and were encamped in the Drau River valley, near Lienz in southern Austria, under the watchful eyes of the British 36th Infantry Brigade. They had hopes that their captors would help them find asylum.

But the British had their orders. On May 26, about 1,500 of the Cossack officers were lured away from the camp on the pretext that they were to meet with British Field Marshal Sir Harold Alexander, a much-respected figure among the Cossacks because he had fought on the side of the czarist White Army against the Bolsheviks in the Russian civil war.

Instead, the officers were arrested and imprisoned. The following morning, they were taken to the town of Judenburg and forced to cross the bridge over the Mur River into Soviet-occupied territory and the waiting arms of the Red Army. The British had carried out their ruse so cleverly that most of the Cossacks had no time to resist. Only a few escaped, but several committed suicide and one jumped off a 100-foot precipice beside the river and was handed over, near death, to the Russians.

In the following days, however, as British troops tried to gather up the remaining Cossacks at various campsites in the Drau valley, they ran into trouble. Now forewarned, the Cossacks and their women and children engaged in passive resistance. In one area near Lienz, several thousand Cossacks congregated early on the morning of June 1 in front of an improvised altar for an open-air Orthodox service conducted by their priests. The British liaison officer, Major W. R. Davies, grabbed a loudspeaker and gave the Cossacks 15 minutes to complete their service before being loaded onto trucks and nearby rail cars. But the singing and praying went on. When the British troops moved in with fixed bayonets to load the Cossacks, Davies recalls, "the people formed themselves into a solid mass, kneeling and crouching with their arms locked around each other's bodies."

The resulting melee lasted nearly four hours before the Cossacks were dragged into waiting trucks and rail cars. Bayonets caused minor wounds, but at least two Cossacks

suffocated. A panic-stricken young woman fled from the crowd and flung her small child and then herself into the Drau River, and several Cossacks were shot to death trying to escape. Here and at other nearby scenes of violence, more than a score of Cossacks died. Within two weeks, though, most of the rest of them had been carted to Judenburg and had crossed the bridge into Soviet captivity.

The fate of the Cossacks after their return was comparable to that suffered by almost all of the estimated 4.5 million other Russians repatriated by the Allies and by the Red Army. A few of the Cossacks from Tolmezzo were tried and executed. The remainder were sent to labor camps where, it has been estimated, more than one half died.

According to an officer of the Soviet secret police who defected to the West many years later, about 20 per cent of all the Russian repatriates were either executed or sentenced to 25 years at hard labor, which amounted to a virtual death sentence. Perhaps only about 15 or 20 per cent of the repatriates returned to their homes unpunished.

As the Soviet Union pursued the process of retribution against its own repatriates during the summer of 1945, concern among the Western Allies about the safety of prisoners shifted to those in Japanese captivity. The Japanese had proved far more fanatical on the battleground than had the Germans, and had fought virtually to the last man as island after island fell to U.S. forces in the Pacific. They also had been far more brutal in their treatment of Allied prisoners. The Japanese still held an estimated 220,000 Allied POWs—140,000 British and Commonwealth citizens, 20,000 Americans and nearly 60,000 Dutch (both military and civilian)—at camps in Southeast Asia, China, Manchuria, the Dutch East Indies and the Japanese home islands.

Japanese attitudes toward defeat and capture—their own and their enemies'—made the future look grim for Allied prisoners. It appeared likely that they would be massacred by their Japanese guards, who would then commit suicide. The portents were particularly ominous early that summer of 1945 in Southeast Asia. What was intended as the final Allied offensive there—the amphibious invasion of Malaya—was scheduled for early September. The Japanese fully expected these landings, as well as an airborne assault on Thailand. They already had orders to meet any offensive with a last-ditch defense that called for fighting to the death and taking Allied prisoners with them.

In Thailand, where the Japanese held 29,000 prisoners who had survived the construction of the "railway of death" in 1942-1943, preparations for this final outcome were painfully evident. The prisoners were forced to dig huge ditches around the perimeters of their camps. These moats were 15 feet deep and 10 feet wide, with machine-gun emplacements at regular intervals. In the event of an Allied invasion, their Korean guards told them, the prisoners would be marched into the ditches and gunned down.

The anxious prisoners would have been glad to know that news of the Japanese intentions had reached the Allies through reports from Thai sympathizers, and that something was being done. In late June, Allied parachute teams began dropping quietly into the mountains and jungles of Thailand, with the double mission of training Thais to rise against the Japanese occupying their country, and to rescue POWs threatened by massacre. These teams, eventually numbering 33 specially trained men, took up positions near the Thailand-Burma railroad and in the areas north and east of Bangkok where many of the prisoners were transferred that summer to help prepare fortifications for the Japanese defenders. Then, supplied by air drops, the parachute teams armed and trained groups of Thai partisans. They also kept a close watch on most of the 11 prison camps in Thailand, ready to move in with their locally trained insurgents at the first hint of mass executions.

Meanwhile, at a camp at Bandung, Java, a South African-born prisoner named Laurens van der Post was also keeping track of Japanese intentions. His information came from a group of friendly Chinese civilians who were allowed to visit the camp to sell food to the prisoners. It was due largely to their efforts that van der Post and the other British and Commonwealth POWs held in the camp were still alive. Simply on van der Post's promise that the British government would repay them after the War, these Chinese had smuggled local currency into the camp. The money enabled the emaciated prisoners to purchase duck eggs, fruit and other commodities through their guards from local Javanese to supplement a starvation diet (by the summer of 1945, their rations had been reduced to slightly over three ounces of rice per day).

But the news brought by van der Post's Chinese contacts

In docile obedience to Emperor Hirohito's surrender order in August of 1945, Japanese from Rota Island in the Marianas line up inside the POW stockade on Guam, 32 miles southwest of their former station.

181

was prized almost as highly as food. Through a connection they never explained to him, the Chinese were in touch with a Korean who had sources of information at Japanese headquarters in Java. Since the beginning of the year, this Korean, known to van der Post only as Kim, had supplied a flow of minor but interesting intelligence that had proved remarkably reliable. In June, for example, Kim had reported that van der Post and the others would be moved from their camp on the Java coast to their present location at Bandung.

Then, in July, Kim brought shocking news. He had seen the secret order from Field Marshal Juichi Terauchi in Saigon, headquarters of the Japanese commander in chief in Southeast Asia, authorizing mass executions of prisoners in the event of Allied invasions. As soon as van der Post heard the news, he launched his preparation. He helped organize the fittest British officers into six platoons of 20 men each. The only available weapons were stones. To arm his men, van der Post arranged with the Japanese to permit the prisoners to gather rocks from outside the camp fence. The pretext he used was that the stones were needed to build drainage gutters in low ground where collecting rainwater created a breeding place for malaria-carrying mosquitoes. To prevent the Japanese, should they decide to do their worst, from catching the prisoners by surprise, a man in each platoon was assigned to stand guard at night.

Only van der Post and a few trusted fellow prisoners knew of Kim's report. Now, their forces armed only with stones, they waited, tuning in every night to Allied broadcasts—from New Delhi, India; Perth, Australia; and San Francisco—on the tiny radio that the British prisoners kept hidden in a pair of wood clogs. Van der Post was certain that only some unforeseen and cataclysmic event could forestall the Japanese intention to kill them all. Unless the Japanese "could be defeated in such a way that they were not deprived of their honor by defeat," he wrote later, "there was nothing but disaster for them and us in the end."

On the night of August 6, the prisoner who had built the radio lay under a mosquito net with his ears pressed to the wood clogs. He had missed the beginning of the broadcast from New Delhi and the reception was bad. He could barely make out the news, as van der Post later put it, that something "had been inflicted on Japan at a place called Hiroshima . . . something new and terrible in human experience."

The radio voice had been so excited that, for a while, the New Zealander suspected he might not have heard the news at all but rather some kind of play—like Orson Welles's 1938 radio dramatization of *War of the Worlds*, which had panicked listeners in the United States with its fictitious reports of an invasion from Mars. The following night, however, the news on the radio was loud and clear: An atomic bomb had devastated Hiroshima.

Van der Post believed that the bombing of Hiroshima, and the subsequent atomic attack on Nagasaki on August 9, were the unforeseen events that would free the Japanese of the shame and dishonor of death and perhaps spare the lives of thousands of Allied prisoners. "This cataclysm," he wrote in *The Prisoner and the Bomb*, "I was certain, would make the Japanese feel that they could now withdraw from the War without dishonor, because it would strike them, as it had us in the silence of our prison night, as something supernatural. They, too, could not help seeing it as an act of God more than an act of man, a Divine intimation that they had to follow and to obey in all its implications."

Whether or not van der Post was right about the influence of the atomic bomb, Emperor Hirohito broadcast to the Japanese people on August 15 his acceptance of an Allied demand for unconditional surrender. The Emperor may have had the Allied prisoners in mind when he warned his subjects, "Beware most strictly of any outbursts of emotion which may engender needless complications." In almost all prison camps on that historic day, the Japanese showed remarkable calm. And they obeyed their Emperor.

Two tragic exceptions to the extraordinarily peaceful manner in which the surrender was accepted occurred in the Japanese cities of Osaka and Fukuoka. At Osaka, a few hours after the Emperor's broadcast, the secret police beheaded more than 50 American airmen being held for interrogation. At Fukuoka, Japanese soldiers vented an explosive rage. They drove 16 U.S. airmen to a slaughtering ground outside town where ritual beheadings of prisoners had been performed twice in the previous two months. Then the Japanese stripped the Americans and hacked them to pieces.

In contrast with the situation in Germany, where prisoners were relieved by the onrushing Allied armies, liberation of the far-flung camps of Asia proceeded slowly. In many camps, several days elapsed before POWs realized that the War was over. Some Japanese commandants could not bring themselves to make the formal announcement. Often the first hint of what had happened came from the suddenly changed behavior of the Japanese guards; they started handing out extra rations, along with Red Cross parcels and letters from home that had been withheld for months and sometimes years. Aware that something was in the wind at his camp in Japan, Australian Roy Whitecross ran a basic test: He knew for certain the War was over when he defied a guard's demand for a piece of cheese that Whitecross had carefully hoarded—and he did not get beaten up.

In the days following Hirohito's announcement of surrender, Allied planes began parachuting rescue teams and tons of food and medicine into the camps. General Douglas MacArthur, the Allied commander, was especially eager to recover one very important prisoner—his old comrade, General Jonathan Wainwright. Since presiding over the surrender of American forces at Corregidor in the Philippines on May 6, 1942, Wainwright had been shunted among a half dozen different camps by the Japanese. He was now believed to be in Mukden, Manchuria, and on August 16, the day after Hirohito's announcement, MacArthur sent a six-man rescue team.

The team found Wainwright at Sian, a camp 100 miles northeast of Mukden. Wainwright, whose longtime nickname was Skinny, was now truly almost a skeleton—130 pounds on a frame of six feet two inches. Harshly treated by his captors, who had sometimes beaten him, he had tried to keep up his spirits by playing solitaire. He was playing game number 8,632 when he heard the War was over. One member of the rescue team, with the assistance of a convoy of Russians who had invaded Manchuria on August 9, took Wainwright to Mukden. There, he was overjoyed to learn that his old boss, MacArthur, had invited him to attend the formal surrender ceremonies aboard the battleship *Missouri* on September 2.

After the surrender, the formal liberation of the prisoners held in Japan still required several weeks. U.S. Occupation forces had to land on all of the islands of the homeland, reach the 176 camps and subcamps, and then transport the former prisoners—about 17,000 men—to hospital ships where they were processed before repatriation. The men

tried to endure the interval as cheerfully as they could.

At Camp Nakarma on Kyushu, the southernmost island of Japan, the 608 British and Commonwealth inmates, all enlisted men, simply took over the camp from their guards and, without any Allied officers there to impose discipline, celebrated their freedom to the hilt. B-29 bombers dropped 40-gallon steel drums full of fruit salad, chocolate and other delights on which the prisoners feasted. Some of the men even hired Japanese civilians as servants, and paid them with food and cigarettes.

A group of Australian prisoners from Camp Nakarma, wearing arm bands identifying them in Japanese as military police, roamed the island by train, popped into restaurants for free meals and confiscated—or traded for—samurai swords. The U.S. Occupation forces had not yet reached Kyushu, and these bold former prisoners were amazed that none of the Japanese showed the slightest sign of hostility; the Australians did not know yet that General MacArthur and Emperor Hirohito had both broadcast warnings to the populace not to harm the prisoners. "We lived like Oriental despots," recalled Kenneth Harrison, "and in many ways I wished that it could go on forever."

At the end of the first week of September, the travels of Harrison and three of his fellow prisoners took them by underwater rail tunnel from Kyushu to the main Japanese island of Honshu. About 10 o'clock in the morning, they left the train and walked into what was left of the city that they had come to see. There, standing ankle-deep in the ashes of Hiroshima, they watched as the burned and scarred people trudged by, and they tried to imagine what it had been like on that day when the bomb burned brighter than a thousand suns.

Harrison, in his three and a half years of captivity, had endured the full brunt of Japanese mistreatment—malnutrition, disease, physical abuse—from the railway of death in Thailand to the coal mines at Camp Nakarma. Others like him would bear mental and physical scars all their lives. But now, as he and his friends surveyed the wasteland of Hiroshima, Harrison felt the years of hatred drain away.

"Poor, poor bastards," muttered one of the men. Then they turned away and began the journey back to the camp that was no longer their prison.

THE SWEET TASTE OF FREEDOM

Ecstatic prisoners of war at Moosburg, Germany, swarm up fences, crowd roofs and mob a barracks square to greet their liberators from the U.S. Third Army.

One of 150 corpses found by American liberators at Davao in the Philippines in June 1945, this POW died of disease or hunger sometime after September 1944

Bundled up in a blanket, a grinning Private Douglas Profitt signs papers that certify his status as an ex-inmate of Bad Orb camp near Frankfurt am Main.

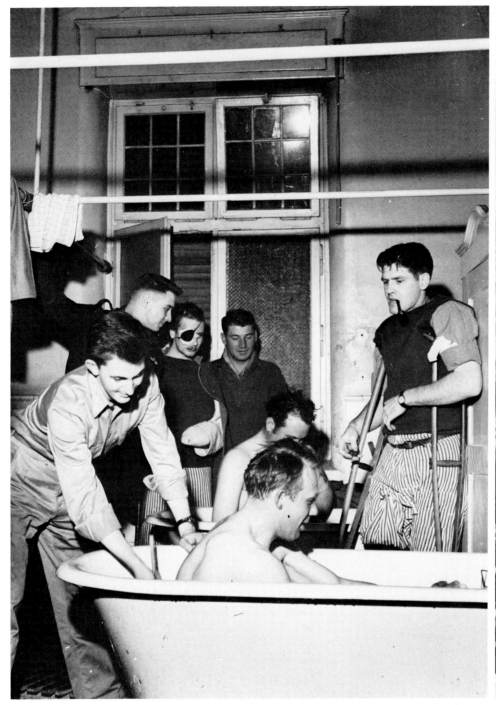

At a prison hospital near Frankfurt am Main, patients and their weary American liberators — one is in the tub — take turns as they enjoy the unaccustomed comfort of a hot bath.

Freed by the advancing forces of the U.S. Ninth Army, British soldiers near Braunschweig in the north of Germany make a festive occasion out of a meal of American rations.

A liberated prisoner winces as a dose of delousing powder is sprayed down the front of his shirt by a U.S. Army medic. Primitive sanitary conditions in some camps led to fear of contracting typhus—a deadly louse-borne infection—and other contagious diseases.

An ambulance team from the U.S. Seventh Army evacuates a stretcher case from Germany's Bad Orb camp, which housed 6,000 Allied POWs at the War's end.

IN THE EAST, A LONG WAIT FOR LIBERATION

For the 220,000 Allied prisoners held in camps within the shattered Japanese Empire, the War ended abruptly: First Hiroshima, then Nagasaki exploded in atomic fire, and on August 15, Hirohito announced his country's surrender. The camp guards laid down their arms and, grudgingly, turned the compounds over to the inmates. But it was a strange kind of liberty. The POWs, often isolated in the deep jungles and weakened by overwork and malnutrition, were in fact helpless. They could only wait patiently for rescue forces to arrive, a process that in some cases took several weeks. "The camps," said one POW, "became prisons without bars. The gates were unlocked, but few of us tried to leave."

One problem was the scale of the victory, which involved liberating huge areas of Asia. Before Japan's surrender, scarcely half a dozen camps had been liberated, most of them in the Philippines early in 1945. There, as the camps fell, the POWs could be quickly and efficiently processed —fed, clothed, counted, examined by doctors and quizzed by intelligence officers—and then sent home on troopships. After the surrender, however, the Allied Occupation forces were faced with the thorny task of taking over the entire Japanese Empire, from Manchuria in the north to Java in the south, with prison camps scattered throughout.

The relief effort took place in two stages. In the first (code-named Operation *Bird Cage*), thousands of leaflets were air-dropped, announcing the surrender and urging all prisoners to stay in their compounds. Then, in the second stage (Operation *Mastiff*), rescue teams as well as food and medical supplies were parachuted into prison camps. To the prisoners, these gifts from the sky were fabulous and often mysterious luxuries. One British doctor, held since 1942, later remembered opening a case of medicines, "some of which I had never seen before: Penicillin baffled me."

The most dramatic event, of course, was the evacuation of the prisons. When that happened, said one POW at Changi camp in Singapore, "we hovered on the brink of tears and laughter, not daring to give way to either for fear we could not stop."

Five days after the surrender of Japan, two Americans freed from Camp Hoten in Manchuria have their pictures taken with their former captors.

Food and medicine arrive by parachute at Bilibid prison in the Philippines in February of 1945; this supply technique was later widely used in Asia.

LIVING SKELETONS OF THE JUNGLE CAMPS

Some of the scenes that greeted the liberators in Southeast Asia were horrifying beyond imagination. At Changi camp in Singapore, the prisoners moved about like shadows, their minds and bodies ravaged by hunger and disease. Captives in some camps had lost more than 100 pounds of their normal weight; it seemed astonishing that men so thin could still live.

As the medical teams set to work examining the survivors, the cost of jungle internment became grimly clear. At least 60 per cent of the POWs suffered from internal parasites, more than half from anemia, 77 per cent from beriberi. Some had gone blind from lack of vitamins, and others had lost arms or legs to ulcerating jungle sores. The doctors did what they could, but many POWs would carry the scars of their ordeal for the rest of their lives.

Australian survivors at Changi camp display artificial limbs of scrap metal and rubber, made by POW medics to replace legs that had turned gangrenous as a result of skin ulcers.

Too weak to rise from their beds in the Changi camp hospital, starved prisoners of war stare blankly in this photograph taken after they were rescued.

One of 150 corpses found by American liberators at Davao in the Philippines in June 1945, this POW died of disease or hunger sometime after September 1944

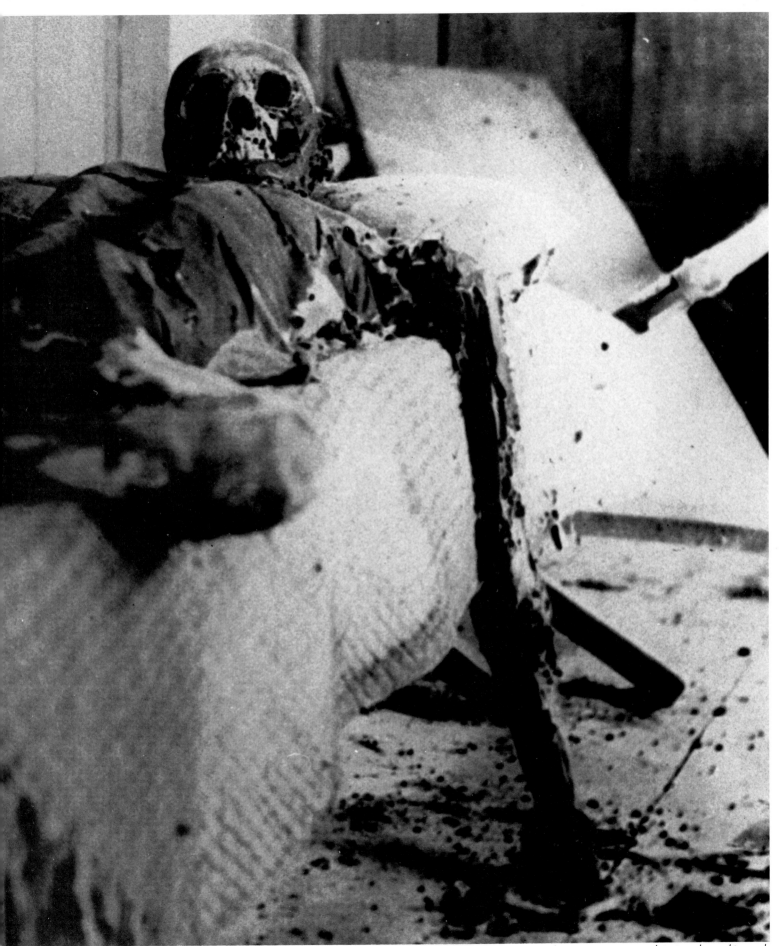

when the Japanese abandoned the camp. Under heavy U.S. bombing, the Japanese took along only prisoners who were strong enough to travel—and to work.

COLD COMFORT IN NORTHERN ASIA

When the liberation forces reached the POW camps in Japan's home islands and in nearby Manchuria, they found conditions tolerable—but barely: Many prisoners had been working at vital jobs in mines or steel mills, and their jailers had at least tried to keep them alive. Even so, the hardships had been awesome.

At Camp Hoten in Manchuria, the worst problem was cold that swept down from Siberia. "We had two seasons there," recalls one survivor, "the Fourth of July and winter." The Japanese guards had cold-weather tunics, but most prisoners had little to wear besides the khakis they had been captured in. Hundreds of POWs contracted tuberculosis and were sent to a hospital that was fitfully warmed by antiquated stoves, each fueled with one scuttle of coal per day.

Rations were one corn muffin and a bowl of soup daily. The men were so debilitated that when they drank their fill of suddenly plentiful kitchen coffee after the camp was liberated, the caffeine made them intoxicated.

Awaiting evacuation from Manchuria's Camp Hoten, a former prisoner douses himself with a bucket of cold water (left). Winter and summer, this was the only way to bathe.

A freed American GI from Camp Hoten bargains for fruit at a nearby market. Many POWs, held in Manchuria since 1942, acquired a working knowledge of the local dialect.

A pair of American prisoner-doctors makes the rounds of Camp Hoten's tuberculosis ward. Water from the bucket in the foreground was splashed regularly across the floor to add needed moisture to the dry, frigid air.

The 10t
NAGOYA M

RATION 10-1 MENU 2

Their ordeal ended, survivors from Camp Fushiki in Japan, and from Cabanatuan in the Philippines (inset), move out on the first leg of their journey home.

BIBLIOGRAPHY

Adams, Geoffrey Pharaoh:
   No Time for Geishas. London: Leo Cooper, 1973.
   The Thailand to Burma Railway. Poole, England: G. P. Adams and the Ashley Press, 1976.
Allan, James, *No Citation.* London: Angus and Robertson, 1955.
Allbury, Alfred G., *Bamboo and Bushido.* London: Robert Hale, 1955.
Anders, Wladyslaw, *An Army in Exile.* London: Macmillan, 1949.
"Army and Navy—Prisoners." *Time,* June 21, 1943.
"Axis Prisoners." *Life,* June 28, 1943.
Bancroft, Arthur, and Rowland G. Roberts, *The Mikado's Guests.* Perth, Australia: Paterson's, 1945.
Barker, A. J., *Prisoners of War.* Universe Books, 1975.
Baron, Richard, Abraham Baum and Richard Goldhurst, *Raid! The Untold Story of Patton's Secret Mission.* G. P. Putnam's, 1981.
Barron, John, *KGB—The Secret Work of Soviet Secret Agents.* Reader's Digest Press, 1974.
Benedict, Ruth, *The Chrysanthemum and the Sword.* Houghton Mifflin, 1946.
Bergamini, David, *Japan's Imperial Conspiracy.* Morrow, 1971.
Berthold, Eva, *Kriegsgefangene im Osten.* Munich: Athenäum Verlag, 1981.
Bethell, Nicholas, *The Last Secret.* Basic Books, 1974.
Blair, Joan, and Clay Blair, *Return from the River Kwai.* Simon and Schuster, 1979.
Borrie, John, *Despite Captivity.* London: Kimber, 1975.
Boyle, Martin, *Yanks Don't Cry.* Bernard Geis, 1963.
Braddon, Russell, *The Naked Island.* London: Werner Lauris, 1952.
Bradley, Omar N., *A Soldier's Story.* Holt, 1951.
Brickhill, Paul:
   Escape or Die. W. W. Norton, 1952.
   The Great Escape. W. W. Norton, 1950.
   Reach for the Sky. W. W. Norton, 1954.
Brown, John, *In Durance Vile.* Rev. and ed. by John Borrie. London: Robert Hale, 1981.
Burt, Kendal, and James Leasor, *The One That Got Away.* London: Collins, 1965.
Burton, Reginald, *The Road to Three Pagodas.* London: Macdonald, 1963.
Butler, J.R.M., ed.: *History of the Second World War—United Kingdom Military Series:*
   Allied Military Administration of Italy, 1943-1945. London: Her Majesty's Stationery Office, 1957.
   The Mediterranean and Middle East, Vols. 1 and 2. London: Her Majesty's Stationery Office, 1956.
Calnan, T. D., *Free as a Running Fox.* Dial, 1970.
Carell, Paul, and Günter Böddeker, *Die Gefangenen.* Frankfurt am Main: Ullstein Verlag, 1980.
Carew, Tim, *Hostages to Fortune.* London: Hamish Hamilton, 1971.
Carr-Gregg, Charlotte, *Japanese Prisoners of War in Revolt.* St. Martin's, 1978.
Castle, John, *The Password Is Courage.* W. W. Norton, 1955.
Chuikov, V. I., *The End of the Third Reich.* Moscow: Progress Publishers, 1978.
Coast, John, *Railroad of Death.* Commodore, 1946.
Cook, Graeme, *Break-Out: Famous Military Escapes of the World Wars.* Taplinger, 1974.
Cooper, Herston, *Crossville: How Did We Treat POWs?* Adams, 1965.
Craig, William, *The Fall of Japan.* Dial, 1967.
Crawley, Aidan, *Escape from Germany.* London: Collins, 1956.
Dallin, Alexander, *German Rule in Russia: 1941-1945.* London: Macmillan, 1957.
Datner, Szymon, *Crimes against Prisoners of War.* Warsaw: Western Press Agency, 1964.
Daugherty, William E., with Morris Janowitz, *A Psychological Warfare Casebook.* Johns Hopkins, 1958.
Davis, Barbara, "POW Nurses: So Proudly We Hail." *The Retired Officer,* March 1974.
Derry, S. I., *The Rome Escape Line.* W. W. Norton, 1960.
Dominy, John, *The Sergeant Escapers.* London: Ian Allan, 1974.
Dulles, Foster Rhea, *The American Red Cross: A History.* Harper and Brothers, 1950.
Durand, Yves, *La Captivité.* Paris: Horizons S.A., 1981.
Eggers, Reinhold, *Colditz: The German Side of the Story.* W. W. Norton, 1961.
Einsiedel, Heinrich von, *I Joined the Russians.* Yale University Press, 1953.
Eisenhower, Dwight D., *Crusade in Europe.* Doubleday, 1948.
Epstein, Julius, *Operation Keelhaul.* Devin-Adair, 1973.
Evans, A. J., *Escape and Liberation: 1940-1945.* London: Hodder and Stoughton, 1945.
Falk, Stanley L., *Bataan: The March of Death.* W. W. Norton, 1962.
Faulk, Henry, *Group Captives: The Reeducation of German Prisoners of War in Britain, 1945-1948.* London: Chatto and Windus, 1977.
Fischer, George, *Soviet Opposition to Stalin.* Harvard University Press, 1952.
Fitzgibbon, Louis, *Katyn.* Scribner's, 1971.
Foot, M.R.D., and J. M. Langley, *MI-9: Escape and Evasion: 1939-1945.* Little, Brown, 1979.
Forrester, Larry, *Fly for Your Life.* Bantam, 1978.
Frank, Benis M., and Henry I. Shaw Jr., *Victory and Occupation: History of U.S. Marine Corps Operations in World War II,* Vol. 5. U.S. Marine Corps, 1968.
Gallagher, J. P., *Scarlet Pimpernel of the Vatican.* London: Coward-McCann, 1967.
Gansberg, Judith M., *Stalag: U.S.A.* Crowell, 1977.
Goerlitz, Walter, *History of the German General Staff: 1657-1945.* Praeger, 1953.
Gordon, Ernest, *Through the Valley of the Kwai.* Harper and Brothers, 1962.
Gordon, Harry, *Die Like the Carp.* Sydney: Cassell Australia, 1978.

Green, J. M., *From Colditz in Code.* London: Robert Hale, 1971.
Greening, C. Ross, and Angelo M. Spinelli with John R. Burkhart, *The Yankee Kriegies.* National Council of the YMCA, no date.
Hall, D.O.W., *Prisoners of Japan.* Wellington, New Zealand: War History Branch, Department of Internal Affairs, 1949.
Halvorsen, David, "American Role in Secret Plot against Hitler Told." *Chicago Tribune,* February 7-13, 1965.
Hancock, Sir Keith, ed., *History of the Second World War—United Kingdom Civil Series:*
   Agriculture. London: Her Majesty's Stationery Office and Longmans, Green, 1955.
   Manpower. London: Her Majesty's Stationery Office and Longmans, Green, 1957.
Hargest, James, *Farewell Campo 12.* London: Michael Joseph, 1945.
Harriman, W. Averell, and Elie Abel, *Special Envoy to Churchill and Stalin: 1941-1946.* London: Hutchinson, 1976.
Harrison, Kenneth, *The Brave Japanese.* Adelaide, Australia: Rigby, 1966.
Hastain, Ronald, *White Coolie.* London: Hodder and Stoughton, 1947.
Hoffmann, Peter, *The History of German Resistance.* MIT Press, 1977.
Huxley-Blythe, Peter J., *The East Came West.* Caxton Printers, 1964.
International Labor Review:
   "The Employment of Prisoners of War in Canada," March 1945.
   "The Employment of Prisoners of War in Great Britain," February 1944.
   "Geneva Convention Regarding Prisoner-of-War Employment," February 1943.
Jacobs, Eugene C., "From Guerrilla to P.O.W. in the Philippines." *Medical Opinion & Review,* August 1969.
James, David, *A Prisoner's Progress.* London: Hollis and Carter, 1954.
The Japanese Story. American Ex-Prisoners of War, Inc.; National Medical Research Committee, Packet No. 10, 1979.
Jaworski, Leon:
   After Fifteen Years. Gulf Publishing, 1961.
   Confession and Avoidance, with Mickey Herskowitz. Anchor Press (Doubleday), 1979.
Kahn, E. J., "Annals of Crime—the Philologist." *The New Yorker,* March 11, March 18, March 25, and April 1, 1950.
Kimball, R. W., *Clipped Wings.* Privately printed, 1948.
Kinvig, Clifford, *Death Railway.* Ballantine, 1973.
Kirby, S. Woodburn, *The War against Japan,* Vol. 5, *The Surrender of Japan.* London: Her Majesty's Stationery Office, 1969.
Kleber, Brooks, "Reflections of an American POW." *Army Newsletter,* May 1981.
Krammer, Arnold, *Nazi Prisoners of War in America.* Stein and Day, 1979.
Kydd, Sam, *For You the War Is Over.* London: Bachman & Turner, 1973.
Leeming, John F., *The Natives Are Friendly.* E. P. Dutton, 1952.
Lewis, George G., and John Mewha, *History of Prisoner-of-War Utilization by the United States Army 1776-1945.* Pamphlet No. 20-213, U.S. Army, 1955.
"*Life* Visits a Prisoner-of-War Camp." *Life,* November 13, 1944.
Littlejohn, David, *The Patriotic Traitors.* London: Heinemann, 1972.
Lumiere, Cornel, *Kura!* Brisbane: Jacaranda, 1966.
McCarver, Norman L., and Norman L. McCarver Jr., *Hearne on the Brazos.* San Antonio Century Press, 1958.
MacDonald, Charles, *The Last Offensive.* U.S. Army, 1973.
Maschke, Erich, ed., *Zur Geschichte der Deutschen Kriegsgefangene das Zweiten Weltkrieges.* Bielefeld, Germany: Ernst und Werner Giesekins, 1974.
Mason, W. Wynne, *Prisoners of War.* Wellington, New Zealand: War History Branch, Department of Internal Affairs, 1954.
Moore, John Hammond, *The Faustball Tunnel.* Random House, 1978.
"Nazis Hoe Cotton." *Business Week,* June 19, 1943.
Neave, Airey:
   Saturday at MI-9. London: Hodder and Stoughton, 1969.
   They Have Their Exits. Little, Brown, 1953.
Pabel, Reinhold, *Enemies Are Human.* Winston, 1955.
Pape, Richard, *Boldness Be My Friend.* London: Elek Books, 1953.
Parkin, Ray, *Into the Smother: A Journal of the Burma-Siam Railway.* London: Hogarth, 1963.
Patience, Kevin, "Guide to the Death Railway." *After the Battle,* No. 26. Ed. by Winston G. Ramsey. London: Battle of Britain Prints, 1979.
Patton, George S., Jr., *War as I Knew It.* Houghton Mifflin, 1947.
Pavillard, Stanley S., *Bamboo Doctor.* London: Macmillan, 1960.
Payne, Robert, *The Life and Death of Adolf Hitler.* Praeger, 1973.
Peacock, Basil, *Prisoner on the Kwai.* London: William Blackwood, 1966.
Pilyar, Yuri, *It All Really Happened.* Moscow: Foreign Publishing House, no date.
Post, Laurens van der, *The Prisoner and the Bomb.* Morrow, 1971.
Pounder, Thomas, *Death Camps of the River Kwai.* Cornwall, England: United Writers Publications, 1977.
"Prisoners: Behind the Wire." *Time,* June 21, 1943.
"Prisoners of War: No Converts?" *Time,* December 11, 1944.
RAMPs: The Recovery and Repatriation of Liberated Prisoners of War. Frankfurt am Main: Office of the Chief Historian, U.S. Army, 1947.
Rawlings, Leo, *And the Dawn Came Up Like Thunder.* Harpenden, England: Chapman, 1972.
Reid, P. R.:
   The Colditz Story. Lippincott, 1953.
   Escape from Colditz. Lippincott, 1973.
   Men of Colditz. Lippincott, 1954.
Reitlinger, Gerald, *The House Built on Sand.* Viking, 1960.

Rivett, Rohan D., *Behind Bamboo*. London: Angus and Robertson, 1950.
Rofe, Cyril, *Against the Wind*. London: Hodder & Stoughton, 1956.
Romilly, Giles, and Michael Alexander, *Hostages of Colditz*. Praeger, 1973.
Russell, Lord Edward, *The Scourge of the Swastika*. Philosophical Library, 1954.
Ryan, Cornelius, *The Last Battle*. Simon and Schuster, 1966.
Shirer, William, *The Rise and Fall of the Third Reich*. Simon and Schuster, 1960.
Simmons, Kenneth, *Kriegie*. Thomas Nelson, 1960.
Smith, Sidney, *Mission Escape*. McKay, 1969.
Solzhenitsyn, Aleksandr, *The Gulag Archipelago, 1918-1956*. Harper & Row, 1973.
Speer, Albert, *Inside the Third Reich*. Macmillan, 1970.
Steenberg, Sven, *Vlasov*. Alfred A. Knopf, 1970.
Streit, Christian, *Keine Kameraden*. Stuttgärt, Germany: Deutsche Verlags-Anstalt, 1978.
Strik-Strikfeldt, Wilfried, *Against Stalin and Hitler*. London: Macmillan, 1970.
Stypulkowski, Zbigniew, *Invitation to Moscow*. London: Thames & Hudson, 1951.
Sullivan, Matthew B., *Thresholds of Peace*. London: Hamish Hamilton, 1979.
Talbot, Strobe, ed., *Khrushchev Remembers*. Little, Brown, 1970.
Thorwald, Jürgen, *The Illusion—Soviet Soldiers in Hitler's Army*. Transl. by Richard and Clara Winston. Harcourt Brace Jovanovich, 1975.
Threadgold, Donald, *Twentieth Century Russia*. Rand McNally, 1959.
Toland, John, *The Last 100 Days*. Random House, 1965.
Toliver, Raymond F., with Hans J. Scharff, *The Interrogator*. Aero, 1978.
Tolstoy, Nikolai, *The Secret Betrayal: 1944-1947*. Scribner's, 1977.
Treaties, Conventions, International Acts, Protocols and Agreements between the United States of America and Other Powers, 1923-1937, Vol. 4. U.S. Government Printing Office, 1938.

Trevor-Roper, Hugh, ed., *Final Entries 1945: The Diaries of Joseph Goebbels*. G. P. Putnam's, 1978.
U.S. House of Representatives, 82nd Congress, 2nd session, *Final Report on Investigation of Katyn Forest Massacre*. U.S. Government Printing Office, 1952.
Urwin, Gregory, "The Road Back from Wake Island." *American History Illustrated*, December 1980.
Veterans Administration Studies and Analysis Service Office of Planning and Program Evaluation, *POW: Study of Former Prisoners of War*. U.S. Government Printing Office, May 1980.
Vietor, John A., *Time Out: American Airmen at Stalag Luft 1*. Richard R. Smith, 1951.
Wainwright, Jonathan M., *General Wainwright's Story*. Doubleday, 1946.
Werth, Alexander, *Russia at War: 1941-1945*. Dutton, 1964.
West, Rebecca, *The New Meaning of Treason*. Viking, 1947.
Whitecross, Roy H., *Slaves of the Son of Heaven*. Sydney, Australia: Dymock's Book Arcade, 1951.
Whittingham, Richard, *Martial Justice*. Henry Regnery, 1971.
Williams, Eric:
   The Book of Famous Escapes. W. W. Norton, 1954.
   Great Escapes Stories. London: Weidenfeld and Nicolson, 1958.
   More Escapers. London: Collins, 1968.
   The Tunnel. London: Collins, 1951.
   The Wooden Horse. Abelard-Schuman, 1958.
Yakulic, George A., "Prisoners of War in Canada." *Canadian Business*, November 1944.
Zawodny, J. K., *Death in the Forest: The Story of the Katyn Forest Massacre*. University of Notre Dame Press, 1962.

PICTURE CREDITS

Credits from left to right are separated by semicolons, from top to bottom by dashes.

COVER and page 1: UPI

THE FACES OF CAPTIVITY—6, 7: Courtesy S.E.A.C., Paris; Black Star; Bulloz, courtesy Musée des deux Guerres Mondiales-B.D.I.C. (Universités de Paris), Paris; Robert Capa from Magnum—Wide World; courtesy S.E.A.C., Paris; G. D. Hackett Collection; UPI.

WAR BEHIND THE WIRE—10, 11: Maps by Diana Raquel Vazquez. 12, 13: U.S. Army, courtesy Eugene C. Jacobs. 15: Australian War Memorial, Canberra (No. 44170). 17: Courtesy Raymond Toliver. 19: *Asahi Shimbun*, Tokyo. 21: Ollie Atkins, Official American Red Cross Photo. 23: Courtesy Betty Rankin.

ORDEAL IN THE FAR EAST—26, 27: Art by Leo Rawlings, courtesy Dr. C. H. Roads, Cambridge, England. 28: Derek Bayes, art by Leo Rawlings, courtesy Dr. C. H. Roads, Cambridge, England. 29: Art by Leo Rawlings, courtesy Dr. C. H. Roads, Cambridge, England. 30, 31: Art by Leo Rawlings, courtesy Imperial War Museum, London. 32: Derek Bayes, art by Leo Rawlings, courtesy Dr. C. H. Roads, Cambridge, England—art by Leo Rawlings, courtesy Wellcome Trustees, London. 33: Art by Leo Rawlings, courtesy Wellcome Trustees, London. 34, 35: Art by Leo Rawlings, courtesy Dr. C. H. Roads, Cambridge, England.

DEATH RAILWAY—38: Map by Diana Raquel Vazquez. 41: Alexander Turnbull Library, Wellington, New Zealand—Australian War Memorial, Canberra. 44, 45: Museum for Education, The Hague, except bottom right, Netherlands State Institute for War Documentation, Amsterdam. 46, 47: Courtesy G. P. Adams Collection, London. 50, 51: Renichi Sugano, Tokyo. 52: UPI.

PRISONERS OF THE REICH—54-56: Angelo M. Spinelli. 57: Courtesy S.E.A.C., Paris. 58, 59: Angelo M. Spinelli; John M. Bennett, courtesy U.S. Air Force Academy Library (4)—Collection Rémy Boutavant, Le Creusot, France; Jean Hoock, courtesy S.E.A.C., Paris. 60-63: Angelo M. Spinelli. 64, 65: Ben Benschneider, courtesy U.S. Air Force Academy Library; courtesy Betty Rankin—Angelo M. Spinelli. 66, 67: Jean Hoock, courtesy S.E.A.C., Paris; Angelo M. Spinelli.

CHANCES OF ESCAPE—71: Imperial War Museum, courtesy S.E.A.C., Paris. 72, 73: Courtesy Richard Kimball, except top right, courtesy Richard Crockatt, Channel Islands. 75, 76: Courtesy Richard Kimball. 77: Art by James Joseph. 78: Courtesy U.S. Air Force Academy Library. 80: Charles Fennell, courtesy J. P. Gallagher, Kent, England—A. C. Cooper, courtesy S. I. Derry, Nottinghamshire, England. 82, 83: Courtesy S.E.A.C., Paris. 84: Stadtmuseum Colditz, courtesy Imperial War Museum, London. 85: Stadtmuseum Colditz, DDR.

BEATING THE SYSTEM—88, 89: Marcel Corre, Vichy, France. 90: Ben Benschneider, courtesy U.S. Air Force Academy Library. 91: Marcel Corre, Vichy,

France. 92, 93: Angelo M. Spinelli. 94: Courtesy U.S. Air Force Academy Library—courtesy Richard Kimball (2). 95: Thomas E. Mulligan Collection. 96, 97: Courtesy Richard Kimball except left, Ben Benschneider, courtesy U.S. Air Force Academy Library. 98: Courtesy Betty Rankin; courtesy Richard Kimball (2). 99: Stadtmuseum Colditz, DDR—Stadtmuseum Colditz, courtesy Imperial War Museum, London (2). 100: Courtesy Richard Kimball. 101: Marcel Corre, courtesy Collection Edmond Petit, Le Vésinet, France.

TREK INTO OBLIVION—102, 103: Archives Documentation Française, Paris. 104: Carl Henrich, Traben-Trarbach, Federal Republic of Germany. 105: Keystone Press, London. 106, 107: Ullstein Bilderdienst, Berlin (West). 108, 109: Bundesarchiv, Koblenz, Federal Republic of Germany; Keystone Press, London, inset, Photo Bibliothèque Nationale, courtesy S.E.A.C., Paris. 110, 111: G. D. Hackett Collection.

CHAOS ON THE EASTERN FRONT—114, 115: Courtesy Boleslaw A. Wysocki. 117: Imperial War Museum, London—G. D. Hackett Collection. 118, 119: Athenäum Verlag, Munich. 120: Süddeutscher Verlag Bilderdienst, Munich. 121: Sovfoto. 122: National Archives (No. 242-HB-47721-306). 123: Ullstein Bilderdienst, Berlin (West). 124, 125: Bundesarchiv, Koblenz, Federal Republic of Germany. 127: U.S. Army.

THE CAPTOR MADE CAPTIVE—130-139: Sovfoto.

AN EASYGOING CUSTODY—140, 141: Edward Clark for *Life*. 142: U.S. Army. 143: Thomas McAvoy for *Life*. 144, 145: U.S. Army, except bottom right, National Archives. 146, 147: Thomas McAvoy for *Life* (2)—National Archives. 148, 149: National Archives—Edward Clark for *Life*. 150: Courtesy Arnold Krammer; U.S. Army—Edward Clark for *Life*. 151: UPI. 152, 153: U.S. Army. 154, 155: U.S. Army, inset UPI.

A PRAGMATIC LENIENCE—159: UPI. 160, 161: U.S. Army. 163: UPI. 164: Keystone Press, London. 167: UPI.

THE ANXIOUS DELIVERANCE—172, 173: Novosti, Moscow. 175: Courtesy U.S. Air Force Academy Library; Imperial War Museum, London. 178: Courtesy David Pollak. 180: UPI.

THE SWEET TASTE OF FREEDOM—184, 185: Courtesy David Pollak. 186: Ben Benschneider, courtesy U.S. Air Force Academy Library. 187: U.S. Army. 188, 189: David Scherman for *Life*; Keystone Press, courtesy S.E.A.C., Paris—courtesy Betty Rankin. 190, 191: U.S. Army. 192, 193: U.S. Army, courtesy Eugene C. Jacobs. 194, 195: Australian War Memorial, Canberra (Nos. 19327 and 19199). 196-199: U.S. Army, courtesy Eugene C. Jacobs. 200, 201: U.S. Army, inset, Carl Mydans for *Life*.

ACKNOWLEDGMENTS

For help given in the preparation of this book, the editors wish to express their gratitude to Geoffrey Pharaoh Adams, Dorset, England; Sadie Alford, Novosti Press Agency, London; Australian War Memorial, Canberra; John Baber, Westchester, Illinois; Musée des deux Guerres Mondiales—B.D.I.C., Paris; John M. Bennett, Bellevue, Nebraska; Peter Breuer, Director, Stadtmuseum Colditz, DDR; Art Bressi, Tucson, Arizona; Pauline Brown, Tampa, Florida; Bureau Soviétique d'Information, Paris; John R. Burkhart, Prescott, Arizona; "Ceux de Rawa-Ruska," Paris; Jeannette Chalufour, Paris; General Albert P. Clark, USAF (Ret.), Monument, Colorado; Richard Coffey, Longboat Key, Florida; Comité International de la Croix-Rouge, Geneva; Marcel Corre, Vichy, France; Mrs. V. M. Destefano, Chief, Reference Library, Defense Audiovisual Agency, The Pentagon, Washington, D.C.; Arthur Durand, Plattsmouth, Nebraska; Yves Durand, Orléans, France; Stanley C. Falk, Chief, Military History, Department of Defense Information Center, Washington, D.C.; C. W. Floody, Toronto; M. R. D. Foot, London; Royal Frey, Curator, and Ruth Hurt, Research Division, U.S. Air Force Museum, Wright-Patterson Air Force Base, Dayton, Ohio; Norihiko Futamatsu, Kyoto, Japan; Isabelle Gautier, Secretary, Camp des Aspirants, Paris; Hermann Glemnitz, Berlin (West); Vito Guido, Dept. of Civil Engineering, Cooper Union, New York City; Werner Haupt, Bibliothek für Zeitgeschichte, Stuttgärt; LaVerne Henderson, Delhi, New York; Arthur Hoen, Shakopee, Minnesota; William Holland, Meridale, New York; Jean Hoock, Paris; Colonel Eugene C. Jacobs, USA (Ret.), Vero Beach, Florida; Major Richard W. Kimball, USAF (Ret.), Bothell, Washington; Harold Kious, Albuquerque, New Mexico; Roland Klemig and Heidi Klein, Bildarchiv Preussischer Kulturbesitz, Berlin (West); Arnold Krammer, Dept. of History, Texas A&M University, College Station, Texas; James Manford, Houston, Texas; Jerome McDavitt, Lake McQueeney, Texas; Françoise Mercier, Institut d'Histoire du Temps Présent, Paris; Samuel Moody, Longwood, Florida; Toshio Morimatsu, Military History Division, Japanese Defense Agency, Tokyo; Thomas E. Mulligan, Delmar, New York; Museum for Education, The Hague; Netherlands State Institute for War Documentation, Amsterdam; Meinrad Nilges, Bundesarchiv-Bildarchiv, Koblenz; Michel Petit, Paris; Hannes Quaschinsky, ADN-Zentralbild, Berlin, DDR; Henry H. and Betty Rankin, Pasadena, Texas; Alain Le Ray, Paris; Duane Reid, Library, U.S. Air Force Academy, Colorado Springs, Colorado; C. H. Roads, Cambridge, England; W. M. Schupbach, Wellcome Institute for the History of Medicine, London; Photographic Department, the Imperial War Museum, London; J. O. Simmonds, Art Department, the Imperial War Museum, London; Marcel Simmonneau, Paris; Margaret Slade, British Red Cross Society, Surrey, England; Helen Smith, Diana, Texas; Stanley Sommers, Marshfield, Wisconsin; Herbert Sorgen, Director, Library, State University of New York, Agricultural & Technical College, Delhi, New York; Angelo M. Spinelli, New York City; General Delmar T. Spivey, USAF (Ret.), Largo, Florida; Wolfgang Streubel, Ullstein Bilderdienst, Berlin (West); Renichi Sugano, Tokyo; George Sweanor, Colorado Springs, Colorado; the Alexander Turnbull Library, Wellington, New Zealand; Fernand Thirion, Secrétariat d'Etat aux Anciens Combattants, Paris; Lt. Col. Patricia Whelan, U.S. Army Office of Public Affairs, New York; Marjorie Willis, BBC Hulton Picture Library, London; Michael Winey, Military History Institute, Carlisle, Pennsylvania; Dr. Boleslaw A. Wysocki, Cambridge, Massachusetts.

The index for this book was prepared by Nicholas J. Anthony.

INDEX

Numerals in italics indicate an illustration of the subject mentioned.